A.R.R.O.W. Tuition

Self-Voice
A Major Rethink

"for Literacy, Speech and
Listening Skill Improvements"

by
Colin Lane

COPYRIGHT
© C.H. Lane 2018 - Ed.4/V.02

All rights reserved. No part of this publication may be reproduced or transmitted in any form or by any means, electronically or mechanically, including photocopying, recording or any information storage or retrieval system worldwide, without prior permission in writing from the copyright owner. Application for the copyright owner's written permission to reproduce any part of this publication should be addressed to the publisher.

Published by A.R.R.O.W. Tuition Ltd.

E-mail: drlane@arrowtuition.co.uk
www.arrowtuition.co.uk

Printed and bound by CPI Group (UK) Ltd, Croydon, CR0 4YY

TRADE MARKS
A.R.R.O.W. and Arrow are registered Trade Marks to the author.
Self-Voice and self-voice are registered Trade Marks to the author.

Dedication

This work is dedicated to Grace Costello, who so loved the written and spoken word.

Acknowledgements

Burden, Professor Robert, School of Education, University of Exeter, three decades of support and advice.

Cleary, Pat, Senior Teacher of the Deaf Somerset, for changing perceptions and delivering vital assistance when needed.

Cole, J, Head of Psychological Service Somerset for continuous help.

Conrad, Dr Reuben, Medical Research Council, Applied Psychology Unit, for inspiration to continue Self-Voice work.

Dickens, Paul, for the patience and effort to improve reading and spelling with A.R.R.O.W. despite illness.

Evans, Dr David, School of Education University of Exeter, whose superb tutoring greatly influenced A.R.R.O.W.'s growth.

Evans, Meurig, Connevans Ltd, for early development support.

Parkes, Barbara, Teacher Baverstock School Birmingham, for advice and total commitment.

Partington, Jim, Stroke. He taught the author much.

Puddy, Bill, Officer with Burnham Carnival Committee for funding the first A.R.R.O.W. recorders.

Ravenscroft, Malcolm, Head Master of Hugh Sexey Middle School Somerset for much needed encouragement and questioning.

Larry, Pupil at Avalon Special School for Children with Moderate Learning Difficulties, Somerset. The presence of a brain tumour did not prevent his enthusiasm for A.R.R.O.W.

All of the above deserve acknowledgement for their contribution to A.R.R.O.W. There are rank upon rank of people alive today who deserve acknowledgement within this work, but unfortunately cannot be named because of the numbers involved. They know who they are.

To everyone deepest thanks, from those you have helped in the past to those you will help in the future.

C.H.Lane

Contents

Copyright ii

Dedication iii

Acknowledgements iv

Introduction 1

Chapter 1 - The Origins of A.R.R.O.W. 3

Chapter 2 - Early Listening and Speech Research 21

Chapter 3 - Research into the Self-Voice 31

Chapter 4 - The Self-Voice, Internal Speech and Learning Attainments 43

Chapter 5 - The Development of A.R.R.O.W. Reading - Spelling Programs . 53

Chapter 6 - Evidence of Literacy Improvements 67

Chapter 7 - The Flexibility of A.R.R.O.W. 83

Chapter 8 - A.R.R.O.W. in the Community 95

Chapter 9 - A.R.R.O.W. in Specialised Sites 121

Chapter 10 - Listening Skill Improvements 133

Appendices 147

References 161

Index 165

Introduction

There is a worldwide need for the raising of standards in literacy and communication. It is widely known that socio-economic expectations are markedly suppressed for people unable to reach, or who have lost, requisite reading, writing, speech and listening skills. This unacceptable situation could be greatly improved for literally millions of children and adults, including those with disabilities, by adopting a teaching/learning system called A.R.R.O.W.

A.R.R.O.W. is an acronym for Aural – Read – Respond – Oral – Write.

Aural …	The student listens to speech on headphones.
Read …	The student reads the text of the spoken material.
Respond …	The student responds to the stimulus.
Oral …	The student repeats the spoken material and this Self-Voice recording then forms the basis of any A.R.R.O.W. work.
Write …	The student writes down what is heard from the recording and marks their own work.

A.R.R.O.W. is a multi-sensory technique. Whilst any one of the A.R.R.O.W. components may be stressed at any particular time, it is the student's own voice, the Self-Voice, which remains central to the approach.

It is acknowledged by the Department for Children Schools and Families, that A.R.R.O.W. achieves, "remarkable if not spectacular results". Latest evidence from across the UK, Ireland and the Caribbean, indeed shows that A.R.R.O.W. is a major contributor within literacy, speech and communication improvement strategies.

This book is a record of several decades work exploring the enormous potential of the Self-Voice to help improve learning and communication skills of children and adults. The population able to benefit from A.R.R.O.W. includes those with Reading, Spelling problems, Dyslexia, Autism, Visual Impairment, Hearing Impairment, Speech and Language Disorder/Delay, Stroke, Traumatic Brain Injury, Cerebral Palsy, Parkinson's, Alzheimer's and other learning and cognitive difficulties. A.R.R.O.W. also helps those of Average and Above Average literacy skills, or for whom English is an Additional Language at Home. The book considers the fundamental role of the Self-Voice, evident even before the development of recording equipment, and its ever widening use as a teaching tool in more recent times.

It is sincerely hoped that the book will encourage fresh avenues of exploration for future researchers and educators, for much remains undiscovered, the journey has just begun.

Chapter 1
The Origins of A.R.R.O.W.

The Self-Voice Experience prior to Recorded Voice Playback 5

On First Meeting the Recorded Self-Voice 6

A.R.R.O.W. The Origins 7

Role of the Voluntary Societies 8

The Equipment – Dual Track Recorders – IT System 8

The Equipment – Headphones 8
    1. Air-Bone Conduction Differences 8
    2. Group Work and Acoustic Distractions 8
    3. Freedom of Movement 9

Pre A.R.R.O.W. Speech/Language Improvement Strategies 9

Speech Clinicians – Others' Findings 9

Negative Attitudes Towards the Self-Voice 9

Parent Positive Attitudes 10

The Rationale Behind A.R.R.O.W. - Use of Prepared Materials 10

Pupils' Reaction and Impact of A.R.R.O.W. 11

Echoing 11

Split Record 12

Echoing and Split Record during Clinical Practice 12
    Example 1 12
    Example 2 12

The Speed of A.R.R.O.W. 13
    Early Organisation of Speech/Language Sessions 13

Speech and Articulation Therapy 14

The Mirror and Tactile Teaching 14

A.R.R.O.W. Early Speech Procedures 14

Traditional 1:1 Speech Procedure 14

Early materials: 15
    Spelling 16
    Poetry 16
    Cine Projector - Cartoon 16
    Visual Display System 17

Economic Advantages of Using A.R.R.O.W. 17

Case Study 18
    Introductory A.R.R.O.W. Work 18
    A Fortnight after Introduction 18
    One Month 18
    Six – Nine Months 19
    Twelve Months 19
    Growing Interest 19

Chapter 1 - Conclusion 20

Chapter 1
The Origins of A.R.R.O.W.

The Self-Voice Experience prior to Recorded Voice Playback
As a 5-6 year old during the mid 1940's, the author would occasionally walk home with his parents and brother John through a passageway between terraced houses in Alcester Lanes End, Birmingham. The author and his brother would sometimes shout a sound close to one of the passageway brick walls in order to hear an almost simultaneous and pleasurable echo effect of their own voices, the Self-Voice. Years later, a teacher of children with sensory and/or learning problems, spoke to the author of a particular child who attended swimming lessons. When in the pool, the child would hold onto the side, placing themselves with an ear close to the wall and shout, as they too, wanted to hear themselves in some form of Self-Voice echo.

At Grammar School during the late 1940's, the author remembers being considerably embarrassed by a teacher of English. With the best of intentions, the teacher unsuccessfully tried to alter several pupils' West Midlands accents. He would ask certain boys, including the author, to stand up from their desks and repeat, "I saw a pound on the ground near the mound". Despite repeated attempts, and laughter from the other boys, the author could not achieve the requested speech pattern. At the time he had no Self-Voice monitoring skills and did not know that he had a strong accent, although he could in fact recognise that people from other regions had different speech patterns. Some 30 years later this lack of Self-Voice monitoring emerged again, but on this occasion with an adult.

Mrs D
A lady from the West Midlands with a local accent helped confirm the lack of Self-Voice monitoring by some adults. She was asked to record a Nursery Rhyme, 'Humpty Dumpty' through an audio cassette recorder linked to a headset boom microphone configuration. The aim was to let her judge her speech before and after hearing it on replay. Prior to the recording exercise, she confirmed that she had never heard herself on tape before. Immediately after recording, but before hearing herself, she was asked what she thought of the quality of the electronic sound system.

"It's lovely Colin using the headsets, very clear."
She was then asked to listen to the recording of Humpty Dumpty played back to her through the headsets. There was a marked negative reaction as Mrs D realised that she had a West Midlands accent.

"I always thought I sounded like my sister in Devon and she sounds like the Queen."

A former rugby player from the Rhonnda, who had represented his country, confirmed that he was unaware of his Welsh accent, albeit well modulated. (Knight, P. 2010)

When moving to the West Country from the Midlands, the author was aware, as a teacher, that his accent would be different to that of children in his new school. Talking to a class of 8 year-old Primary School children he explained that he had moved from another part of England. A child with a marked Somerset burr responded:

"Oh we know you don't come from round here, you speak much funnier than we do".

From the examples given, it is apparent that there are several forces at work when producing speech. Initially, these involve a subliminal following and "live", reproduction of a regional accent and some form of checking apparatus ensuring that this pattern of speech is being maintained. These processes however, seemingly operate quite independently of the ability to detect different accents in others. There are considerable implications regarding these factors when teaching literacy and communication skills using A.R.R.O.W. Self-Voice, as implied criticism or alteration of a child's poor speech pattern, cannot assume that the child is in fact aware of their deviant production.

On First Meeting the Recorded Self-Voice

During the mid 1950's, whilst in the 6th Birmingham Company Boys' Brigade, the author first met the recorded Self-Voice. Ken, an enterprising officer of the company, asked a group of elder boys, to speak into a reel-to-reel tape recorder and listen back to their recordings. The effect was dramatic. All of the boys, including the author, clearly showed a high degree of interest, liking and some form of Self-Voice recognition after the first replay - students meeting the replayed Self-Voice today, still show the same characteristics.

Over ten years later, experimental American work by Rousey and Holzman (1967), underlined that there was a marked reaction upon hearing the Self-Voice, in terms of psychological and physiological responses. During this period, some recording artists in the entertainment world sang "live" in unison with descant recordings of their own voices. The American singer Kay Starr, recorded two harmonies on the record "Side by Side" and the Liverpool-born performer Michael Holliday often interacted with a recording of his voice during stage or television performances. Despite the pioneering American research by Rousey and Holzman (Ibid) and novelty value of the Self-Voice in popular music, there was, according to the literature, little, if any, intensive use of the recorded Self-Voice for literacy or speech improvement in the early and mid 1960's.

During the 1960's, tape recorders became more available and in some schools were used, not only for replaying music or broadcasts, but also as an aid to help reading. Groups of children would listen through a bank of headphones to 'home produced' recordings made by a teacher and based upon designated reading scheme books. In some cases, the children would be required to write out answers from teacher-designed comprehension sheets. At this time however, tape recorder work did not appear to use the child's own voice, the Self-Voice, as a means of improving reading, spelling and language skills. The author's first experience of the educational potential of tape recorders was at Ipsley County Primary School Redditch, at the time a 'jewel in the crown' for Worcestershire schools in terms of English teaching and Music. A small stream ran at the bottom of the school playing field. This stream was a feeder to the River Arrow flowing through both Worcestershire and Warwickshire and this link partly helped determine the acronym A.R.R.O.W.

A.R.R.O.W. The Origins

The working origins of A.R.R.O.W. began in 1974, in a Unit for Hearing-Impaired children in Somerset where the author was employed as Teacher of the Deaf. The teaching of speech, language and auditory skills was at that time, the responsibility of the Teacher of the Deaf who was either based within a mainstream school as a Unit Teacher, or worked as a peripatetic teacher, visiting clusters of mainstream schools which had one or more Hearing Impaired pupils included within their total population. When in the author's Unit, most of the Hearing Impaired children he saw received daily 1:1 speech/language tuition. There was during this period, little information in the literature, about a tightly structured use of the child's Self-Voice in order to improve speech/language skills. The use of audio-tapes and audio-card players, in which of course, both teacher and child voices could be recorded, nevertheless suggested that future Self-Voice work could be a worthwhile educational exercise.

In 1974, the author was aiming to improve his French at evening class. The evening class used reel-to-reel two track language laboratory equipment as part of the learning programs. The equipment played a French voice through headsets linked to associated French text. Students were required to repeat the French sample and listen back to both the French voice and their own on replay. The author immediately noticed the novelty and heightened interest in his own replayed voice in addition to the French voice he was copying. It seemed to him that it would be beneficial to let Hearing Impaired children experience the same facility in order to improve their speech and language skills. An English company, Connevans Ltd, who still today market equipment for the Hearing Impaired, were also at the time, manufacturing language learning equipment. Connevans developed a link between their language laboratory equipment and a high amplitude auditory trainer. This link gave the Hearing Impaired children within the Unit a greater opportunity to hear their own recorded voice at optimum volume and with necessary frequency adjustments. Given the availability of daily 1:1 teaching and access to high fidelity amplifying/recording equipment, a unique opportunity emerged for focusing on Self-Voice work.

Role of the Voluntary Societies

During the early developmental period, Voluntary Societies in the region were approached in order to help purchase the specialist equipment. They responded most generously to what was essentially experimental work. The societies included Carnival Clubs, The Lions, Round Table, local National Deaf Children's Societies and Inner Wheel. At the time, some educators felt A.R.R.O.W. Self-Voice work was contentious. Somerset County Council however, admirably gave full support to the A.R.R.O.W. concept, once they saw the positive effects upon their Hearing Impaired children.

The Equipment – Dual Track Recorders – IT System

A feature of the early development period and indeed the current A.R.R.O.W. approach, is the use of a dual track recorder. Initially, A.R.R.O.W. used reel-to-reel recorders which were then refined to audio cassette systems. Both the reel-to-reel and later audio cassette recorders, were used in parallel with hard copy books in order to present pre-recorded text for the student to read and repeat. A.R.R.O.W. has further refined its materials and now utilises digital computer technology for recording, replay and on-screen text. The dual track facility allows the student to listen to a voice, copy it by speaking, then have the option to replay both voices whilst looking at the text. The Tutor voice never erases - the student track erases each time a new recording is made. The A.R.R.O.W. IT system therefore, allows many students in turn to use the same computers and software material.

The Equipment – Headphones

An important feature of A.R.R.O.W. is the use of high fidelity recording/replay equipment using headphones. Headphones offer several advantages over hand held microphone recordings played back by air conduction:

1. Air-Bone Conduction Differences

Usually, when talking, we hear the sounds of our own speech through bone conduction within our head as well as through our ears. We do not normally hear the sounds of other peoples' speech through bone conduction, but through air conduction transmitted via the ear canal, middle ear ossicles and auditory nerves to the brain. The difference between listening to the Self-Voice through bone conduction and listening to the Self-Voice solely through air conduction, causes an identification discrepancy for some people. The discrepancy exists as a result of what people expect to hear and what they do, in fact, hear. The voice as spoken and replayed in a recording via headphones however, moves far closer to a 'speak and listen' match, than when listening, through air conduction alone, to a Self-Voice recording. There is additionally, an acoustic immediacy effect when using headphones, both in the recording and replay mode, which proves very important to speech/language work.

2. Group Work and Acoustic Distractions

A second and very practical use of headphones, is the privacy it allows the student when working alone or in groups. The pupil can record the Self-Voice, replay it as part of literacy or communication improvements and minimise the distraction effects from, or to, nearby students. Headphones enable students to work in less than ideal acoustic conditions including those classrooms in which other activities are being undertaken.

3. Freedom of Movement
When listening and recording using headphones, students can work hands-free. The hands-free facility gives the student greater flexibility in terms of undertaking written work or A.R.R.O.W. recording and replay processes.

Pre A.R.R.O.W. Speech/Language Improvement Strategies
It was established well before the development of A.R.R.O.W. that Hearing Impaired students could improve speech/language skills through auditory training and speech rehabilitation. The remediation work however, was usually based upon systematic and somewhat lengthy processes. These would often require a high degree of tutor skill and student co-operation when undertaking training. The most widely accepted method of teaching speech and listening skills to groups of Hearing Impaired Children, was based upon Look Read Speak (LRS). The LRS approach was teacher directed and used an overhead projector with text on screen. The teacher faced the children and read text which could be either a word, phrase, sentence or group of sentences. The teacher then asked the pupil(s) to repeat either a word, phrase, sentence or group of sentences from the text. Having worked through the passage, the teacher masked the text with a sheet of paper and required the pupils to identify appropriate words, phrases or sentences spoken to them. The teacher would sometimes mask their lips in order to heighten the child's reliance upon auditory awareness when trying to determine which part of the passage or word they had just heard.

Speech Clinicians – Others' Findings
When the author was in the process of exploring the use of the Self-Voice as a teaching tool, he could find little evidence of published research by speech clinicians on either side of the Atlantic, on how to use the tape recorded Self-Voice for speech and communication improvement. In fact, many educators doubted the benefits of using and manipulating recordings of the Self-Voice in order to improve speech/language skills. Prior to A.R.R.O.W., the replayed taped Self-Voice had therefore, mainly been used as a tool to demonstrate faults in speech production, not as a 'positive' model upon which further improvements could be based.

Negative Attitudes Towards the Self-Voice
The non-A.R.R.O.W. negative use of the Self-Voice, as an illustrator of errors,

parallels commonly held views at that time:

- "I don't like my voice when I hear it."
- "I don't recognize my voice when I hear it."
- "What is the point of playing poor speech back?"

Much of the author's initial A.R.R.O.W. work therefore, was innovative and based upon personal experience using trial and error, in which successful strategies were retained and unsuccessful ones were discarded.

Parent Positive Attitudes

After a few months of children commencing A.R.R.O.W. Aural, Read, Respond, Oral, Write work, parents became enthusiastic about the speech and listening improvements...

"Quote what you will, absolutely fantastic."
V Willoughby
"Very impressive indeed." Mrs D Ireland
1976 'Talk' No 79 National Deaf Children's Society pp 19-20
"Before I would call him from upstairs and he wouldn't hear me, now he can."
S Manley HTV Points West 1987 News Item

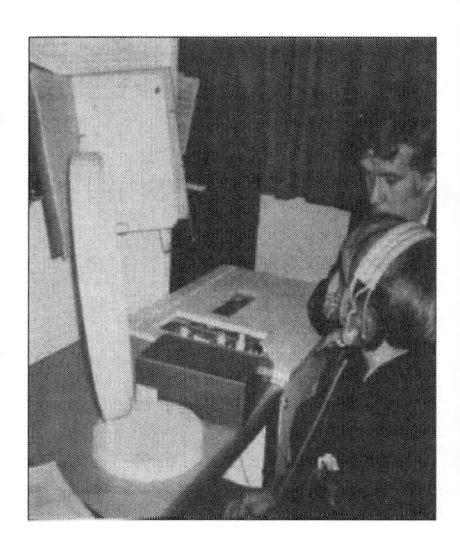

There was clearly a difference between the generally accepted views of educators who had not investigated A.R.R.O.W. and the initial response from children using the approach and their parents. Any less-than-positive attitudes about the worth of Self-Voice work, were to be later challenged by clinical evidence and research with school-age pupils.

The Rationale Behind A.R.R.O.W. - Use of Prepared Materials

The focus of A.R.R.O.W. Self-Voice training in the early days, was that students would learn to improve their communication skills by listening to a master recording on tape, which was linked to text in a book. The format and effects of using the book are discussed in more detail later in this chapter, but in essence, the student would listen to the tape, look at both text and illustrations in the book, copy the tape by speaking and listen back to both tutor and student taped voices before writing out the text. In essence, the student would try to emulate the teacher voice in order to improve their own speech or language skills. Throughout the 1:1 procedure, the teacher held a central position both as controller, conversation partner, and adviser to the child in terms of speech improvement and language growth. The overall A.R.R.O.W. strategy was based on the major assumption that the student recognised their error patterns when comparing these to the Tutor's voice and also knew they had a speech problem. These assumptions, made not only by the author, but by other Teachers of the

Deaf who were contacted about the Self-Voice, were later challenged by A.R.R.O.W. research projects.

Pupils' Reaction and Impact of A.R.R.O.W.
Within a few weeks of meeting A.R.R.O.W. several effects became evident which enhanced the original listen, compare, improve strategy. These effects are still evident today:

- The students showed they preferred listening to their own replayed voice rather than the tutor's recording. Some students in fact, turned off the Tutor voice on replay.
- On many occasions, students smiled when first hearing their own replayed voices but never smiled when listening to the author's.
- Some students also gave an indication of some link with the internalising processes by silently mouthing their Self-Voice speech sample when it was presented to them on playback.
- The students voluntarily lowered the amplitude at which they preferred to listen to the speech pattern, i.e. they had improved their auditory attention skills - the vital art of listening.
- The faster the replay of the Self-Voice, the greater the impact upon the reinforcement of speech/language patterns.
- The children almost immediately showed that they could practise A.R.R.O.W. speech and language work independently. The tutor or assistant therefore, assumed the role of facilitator and was able to overview groups of students using the approach.
- The system allowed large numbers of Special Needs students to benefit, thereby enabling the Unit to operate with a highly cost effective Specialist teacher-pupil ratio when compared to other speech/language/literacy methods.

Two techniques evolved from early clinical practice which had a lasting influence upon the A.R.R.O.W. Self-Voice learning techniques, viz. Echoing and Split Record.

Echoing
It is known that immediate feedback, reinforcement and repetition, can be most positive influences towards the acquisition of skill learning. The author immediately observed that the intuitive use of a student's voice being rapidly and repeatedly replayed as confirmation of progress, often caused more effective learning than a delayed, single replay. A technique called "Echoing" was therefore developed in which improved speech or language structures were quickly replayed within 2-3 seconds after being recorded. It soon became apparent that the benefits of Echoing, were not only to confirm progress, but also to maintain the speech signal within the auditory echoic memory system. Later research into the Self-Voice endorsed the many advantages of using Echoing as a short term auditory store of a required utterance.

Split Record

The Split Record technique, is one in which a previously unobtainable speech pattern is rehearsed in obtainable sections which are then recorded one section at a time. These recordings are afterwards replayed as a fluent utterance, often with an almost indiscernible gap between the individually practised components. The text material is also used as an additional stimulus. It was observed that students sometimes silently mouthed structures recorded through this technique, even though they had previously found them unpronounceable because of ineffective linguistic processing or poor articulatory skills. In some way, A.R.R.O.W. Split Record greatly enhances a link with the internalising processes and illustrates how the word or phrase is supposed to be spoken. It seems evident that when utilising Split Record, the brain effectively stores the material in its correct format, guided by the strong multi-sensory link and power of the echoed voice. The phonological input of the Self-Voice is thus linked to the content of the recorded material, be it Topics or Spellings. The dynamic link between the auditory, visual and kinaesthetic input of the written word, helps establish a permanent learning effect with the student. The result is that a student is able to write and read more successfully than previously.

A 10 year old Dyslexic boy states:
"It's good, it like injects it into your brain straight away and it's fun…"

A male dyslexic, 18 year old student summarises A.R.R.O.W.:
"It's brilliant, it brings everything together around my own voice."

Echoing and Split Record during Clinical Practice
Example 1

If a student has articulation or sequencing problems, a combination of Echoing and Split Record can be a potent teaching agent. During an early demonstration of A.R.R.O.W. a child with communication problems could not produce the final sibilant "s" on the word "cats" in the sentence "The cats are here" and kept perseverating with "The cat are here".

Two strategies were employed.

1. The sentence was recorded in two sections, notably the words "The cat" followed by the lengthy "ssar here". A judicious use of the Pause/Record control meant the two sections were blended together on replay to produce "The cats are here".
2. The complete sentence was replayed several times as the student both heard the target pattern using his Self-Voice whilst also seeing the written format "The cats are here".
   The child gave the correct utterance almost immediately.

Example 2
Many years after this demonstration, one of the newly trained teachers from Waterford, Southern Ireland began working 1:1 with a Travellers' child. The

pupil was six years of age and was experiencing a severe language deficit. The teacher was hoping to improve language skills using cartoon based cards and began to use A.R.R.O.W. as part of each teaching session. During a session, the teacher showed a cartoon card and spoke a single word relating to the image on the card. Prior to A.R.R.O.W. the child could copy the teacher saying the word, but she could not spontaneously give the appropriate word to the cartoon without teacher input, i.e. unless she was copying the teacher's model. Using A.R.R.O.W. the teacher showed the six year old the card of a boy smiling and managed to record the child saying, "happy". This was echoed back to her several times and eventually the child repeated, "happy" when she was shown the card. The same Self-Voice procedure was followed for the word, "hungry". After echoing, the girl again gave the word, "hungry" appropriately, purely by looking at the cartoon.

The next day she was shown the cards and again said, "happy" and "hungry", according to whichever card was shown to her. The third successive day, she again correctly uttered "happy" and "hungry" when shown the appropriate picture. A.R.R.O.W. echoing had obviously resulted in some learning effect with the little girl and she had internalised to her mental dictionary the two words, "happy" and "hungry", after listening to herself saying those words. From this baseline, the teacher plans to add more single words to her vocabulary.

The Speed of A.R.R.O.W.
The overall speed of the master voice and child recall and comparison is impressive. A series of five simple words, phrases or sentences, e.g. 'Horses', 'A horse', 'A brown horse', 'A quiet horse', 'A happy horse', 'A horse in a field', can be attended to, recorded, and recordings checked, inside 1 minute. Within 60 seconds a child has therefore, heard 6 correct master recordings of sentences, has responded 6 times and heard both responses 6 times. If the child's pattern is originally correct, 24 positive auditory imprints have occurred within 60 seconds.

Early Organisation of Speech/Language Sessions
During the early A.R.R.O.W. sessions there was much 1:1 work with pupils on a daily basis. Each Hearing-Impaired pupil was seen for speech and/or language improvement. Sessions lasted some 10-15 minutes per day and where required, pupils could receive two sessions each day. This pattern was followed for several years, involving the author in an estimated 1500 hours working A.R.R.O.W. with Hearing Impaired pupils. This amount of 1:1, with a relatively small number of students, resulted in an ever widening experience of using Self-Voice strategies.

Within a few weeks of introducing the new technologies, it became apparent that the system enabled pupils to undertake speech and listening practice on their own, whilst under the overall supervision of a Teaching Assistant. It also became evident that the pupils, when practising, realised standards of speech often equivalent to that obtained when undertaking help from the author, as a Teacher of the Deaf.

Speech and Articulation Therapy

The replay of a student's own voice became an integral part of speech/language improvement processes. Within a 10 minute speech/language session, the Self-Voice may only have been used for some 2 minutes. During that short 2 minute period however, there had been a continuous amount of recording and Self-Voice replay using Echoing and Split Record, in order to confirm and further advance speech and language progress.

Articulation therapy, conducted on a 1:1 basis, centred upon words or phrases which were later included within a carrier sentence. Therapy was undertaken with the recorder set on 'Record' but in the 'Pause' mode so that an immediate record process could be met simply by coming off 'Pause'. If no improvement resulted, the phoneme was again practised either alone or within a word. Remediation of an individual sound was attempted only if failure occurred within a sentence or single word context. Any improvements in articulation, were immediately replayed by Echoing after being uttered, thereby maintaining the sound within the cortex and also acting as a confirmation of progress. The Echoing effect therefore, has its roots in both the neurological and psychological modalities.

The Mirror and Tactile Teaching

A key piece of equipment during articulation therapy, was a stand-alone mirror allowing the pupil and tutor to see that correct tongue positions and face patterns were being effected by the pupil. The student was also helped to produce appropriate speech patterns by demonstration and assistance from the author which used touch and/or tongue positioning during speech improvement sessions.

A.R.R.O.W. Early Speech Procedures

A transcript analysis of an A.R.R.O.W. 5 minute lesson, aiming to improve a child's sibilant 's' production, reveals the main emphasis is one of self-voice involvement (Lane 1980, pp 106-111). During the 's' therapy session, the tutor made 13 utterances. The child made 15 utterances and had her own Self-Voice improved patterns replayed back 32 times. Out of the total conversation flow there was a 78% involvement by the child in Self-Voice listening, either when firstly speaking, or secondly, when listening back to her own recordings. A high proportion of the session therefore, involved the student in listening to her own voice giving improved approximations to the master recording. The taped material used during the session was then available for the child to practise on a separate occasion(s), when her involvement in the listening and speech skills would be replicated.

Traditional 1:1 Speech Procedure

A comparison was made against a more 'traditional' approach delivered by an independent speech clinician. The traditional lesson, again aiming to improve an 's' production, showed the child was not able to be so involved in Self-Voice listening. In the five minute traditional session, the child heard herself giving 20 utterances from a total of 57 made during the conversation flow. Her Self-Voice involvement was therefore 35% of the overall utterance total, of which only a minority of examples contained improved 's' target sound examples. The speech clinician made 37 utterances from the 57 given, and therefore dominated the conversation. Additionally, the tutor was channelled into constantly switching her own linguistic utterances in order to negate boredom and maintain the child's interest when attempting to improve speech production. The pattern switching caused the child to constantly face read the teacher for language information. This face reading task drew much attention away from the task of pre-planning and producing 's' sounds within speech.

The tutor using A.R.R.O.W. therapy was better able to prepare for the task of assessing the child's production, because he was not so heavily involved in generating improved patterns. Using the traditional non-A.R.R.O.W. method, the child would not have heard so many regular, improved models even when practising alone.

It should be pointed out, that A.R.R.O.W.'s flexibility allows it to be used within a conventional speech/language approach, albeit for a rapid, dynamic, short period of time, perhaps lasting only a few minutes, before moving on to other tasks within a session.

Early materials:
An illustrated text book and pre-recorded tapes were produced by the author. The format for the book was influenced by program-learning techniques which he had met during teacher training in 1965.

The early A.R.R.O.W. programs contained some 300 basic sentence and question patterns which also used all the vowels consonants and diphthongs in English transcribed into phonetic symbols in the index. The sentences varied in length and complexity but were mainly based upon a simple active declarative format. An individual sentence with its response space was given three times on tape. Written work involved in the book used simple correct word slotting in a sentence (cloze procedures), choosing correct words from a given collection, or writing sentences around a given word. An early indication of the power of A.R.R.O.W. soon became evident. A severely Hearing Impaired child uttered, without prompting, a simple sentence he had practised in the A.R.R.O.W. book, "The man is up the pole". The sentence was spoken by him as he was being driven past a workman repairing wiring on a telegraph pole. It was the first time he had been observed to spontaneously utter a sentence containing appropriate syntax.

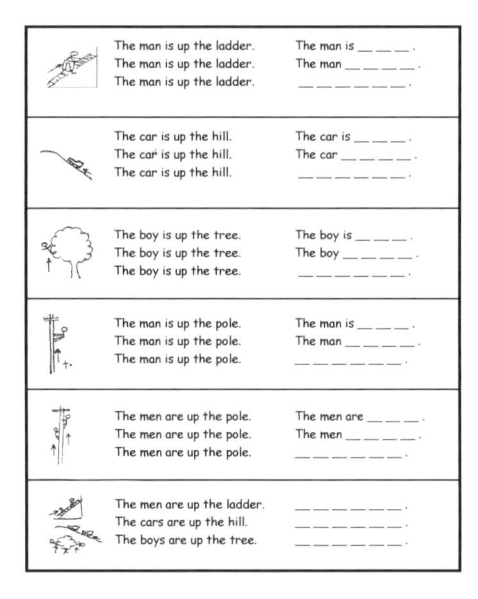

Spelling

Additional material included spellings and their use within sentences. The roots of the A.R.R.O.W. spelling technique began at Ipsley County Primary School in 1967, using a Teacher recorded voice and 'home' produced work cards for a group of 8 pupils who were linked through a bank of headphones to a tape-recorder. The children listened to the teacher voice saying a word/spelling and took dictation from the adult example. There was however, no Self-Voice input.

The Spelling approach used at Ipsley County Primary School, was further refined for use with A.R.R.O.W. Hearing Impaired pupils some 8 years later, when they began to listen back to their own voices speaking 30 phonetically balanced lists of spellings to be learnt. It should be placed on record that in the early years of the Hearing Impaired Unit work, spelling assumed a lesser teaching priority than speech, listening and language skills. After early experimentation, mainstream students based in the host Middle School who were themselves experiencing literacy problems, also began to use A.R.R.O.W. most successfully.

Poetry

Selections of poems and limericks were prepared for use with A.R.R.O.W. These selections left a time interval between each line, allowing the child to copy and compare the pre-recorded master line. It was noted that an 8 year old child with a substantial hearing loss spent up to 15 minutes at a time practising poetry. Whilst undertaking this A.R.R.O.W. literacy based task, the student was of course also undertaking a series of audio and speech improvement programs central to the approach and later replicated in the 21st century IT programs.

Cine Projector - Cartoon

In 1976, films and written/recorded commentaries were simultaneously linked within the A.R.R.O.W. approach. The child saw a moving film, heard a commentary linked to the text of the movie and repeated this as the action of the film progressed. The child therefore, gained experience of specific language patterns linked to film movements.

One severely language impaired girl pupil, 11 years of age, made a 27% improvement in speech (vocalisations) after 7 practice sessions (Ibid, 1976). Three years later, a more stringent research project showed that vocalisation skills improved as a direct consequence of using the 'standard' A.R.R.O.W. approach involving the written and spoken word, without recourse to a moving image. The successful use of the early cine-projector A.R.R.O.W. work, was to lead however, some 25 years later, to the introduction of the very important movie facility within the computer based program.

Visual Display System

An oscilloscope waveform visual display system, was linked to an A.R.R.O.W. recorder. In effect, when the students spoke, a moving wave pattern was simultaneously shown on screen. The waveform would move according to the sentence, phrase or speech sound being produced. Vowels would be shown as a low regular pattern. Consonants would be shown as various peaks and it was easy to differentiate between a vowel and consonant and/or voice intensity in running speech. Using a pause facility, the student could look at the master recording waveform and compare this to the student version. It was found that Hearing Impaired pupils gained considerable benefit and encouragement to practise, sometimes on their own, when using a visual display system linked to A.R.R.O.W. The oscilloscope type facility is being investigated within a specially developed IT program and offers another alternative within the overall speech improvement series of techniques.

In a very early article the author summarised the overall impact of A.R.R.O.W.
"The comparison approach has been used in Somerset some 7 months. There has been a marked improvement in the speech of the children, particularly those able to identify the sounds of speech by amplification and frequency cuts, it has considerably altered the teaching of speech and the results obtained."
Lane 1975 Journal of the Society of Teachers of the Deaf Issue 20 pp 17-20.

Economic Advantages of Using A.R.R.O.W.

After twelve months, a bank of four A.R.R.O.W. systems were operating in the Hearing Impaired Unit. One was used within a Speech Room for specialist based work. The other three systems were sited in the main classroom and were used for Speech/Language revision or mainstream curriculum based work. The level of A.R.R.O.W. differed from pupil to pupil according to age, ability and curriculum requirements.

Pupils were able to work independently on A.R.R.O.W. by meeting 30 minute curriculum-based Topics covering Science, History, Geography and Maths. Comprehension questions were met as part of each Topic. The system proved most effective on several counts:

- Pupils could receive preparation or follow-up work on curriculum based programs
- Speech and Listening Skills were also being reinforced when undertaking A.R.R.O.W. curriculum-based Topics
- Groups of up to four students could operate with an overviewing assistant in the main room, whilst the Teacher of the Deaf could work with an individual pupil on personalised Speech/Language programs within an adjoining speech room

Several decades later an independent Eire survey (Nugent 2012), explored the economic advantages of various literacy interventions. The project found that A.R.R.O.W. was the most effective in terms of training time/results because of the numbers of pupils per teacher able to work on the system.

A carousel system for both pupils and support staff, enabled some 23 students to follow a carefully structured inclusion system within the Mainstream School/ Hearing Impaired Unit. Two/three teaching assistants supported pupils, either within the mainstream school or in the Unit and a part-time non-specialist teacher worked in the Unit in conjunction with the Teacher of the Deaf. The staffing ratio for these students was, at the time, well below the recommended norm of one Specialist Teacher of the Deaf for each 3-4 Hearing Impaired students within a school. The financial savings, due in no small manner to the application of A.R.R.O.W. in the Unit, were considerable.

Case Study
Lane 1978 the Volta Review Volume 80 No.3 pp 149-154

Jeffrey was introduced to A.R.R.O.W. as an 8 year old severely deaf, hyperactive child with minimal concentration ability, unintelligible speech, and no receptive language understanding, unless mime and gesture were used. Expressive language, either through speech or writing, was non-existent.

Introductory A.R.R.O.W. Work
Initially, 5-10 minutes daily remediation was given, using A.R.R.O.W. equipment, book and pre-recorded tapes. Jeffrey used an auditory trainer capable of delivering high amplitude and appropriate frequency cuts. Early emphasis was given to the rhythmic association of speech. Each session commenced with familiarising Jeffrey with the text and the accompanying line drawings. Acceptable responses were replayed and randomised for auditory discrimination. After each therapy session, Jeffrey was required to reproduce the practice structures using his body-worn hearing aid. Written follow up work was initiated. Jeffrey, unprompted, attempted rhythm modification after Tutor Self-Voice comparison during his first A.R.R.O.W. session. Some partially hearing children showed that they were capable of identifying articulatory errors on first replay. Using A.R.R.O.W., Jeffrey soon gained confidence and increased concentration.

A Fortnight after Introduction
It was found that Jeffrey could undertake independent daily practice. The concentrated audio involvement minimised face reading and constant reference to the written word. During practice sessions an overviewing teaching assistant reported any persistent regression from improvements initially gained during A.R.R.O.W. 1:1 therapy.

One Month
After 4 weeks, it was noted that Jeffrey had a positive A.R.R.O.W. attitude. He could identify, without using face reading, randomised sentences from the A.R.R.O.W. book. He recognised rhythm, syntax and vocabulary deviations by voice replay and reference to the written patterns. Alternative examples to

'speech practice' material were generated by him. Simple A.R.R.O.W. processed poetry was recorded and practised. It was felt that the inherent auditory training, speech skills and self sufficiency encouraged in him when he practised alone, outweighed the dangers of any poor speech patterns he made being reinforced on replay.

Six – Nine Months
After 6 months, single sentence modifications against cartoon pictures were first attempted. Sequences up to 8 sentence length were being produced and replayed to him. Jeffrey could, by audition alone, obtain up to 100% success in randomised sentence recall without reference to any text. Observations after 9 months revealed that Jeffrey's practice A.R.R.O.W. material was 80% intelligible to uninitiated listeners, and his running speech had a definite rhythmic quality. All of Jeffrey's expressive language stemmed from A.R.R.O.W. material which was transferred to other situations. He could verbally understand and communicate in writing, simple statements, questions and commands.

Twelve Months
During the commencement of his second year, therapy was maintained and increased to 30 minute daily A.R.R.O.W. work. More complex material was introduced. Jeffrey still preferred to listen to his own recordings when undertaking dictation. He was able to spend 50% of working time unsupervised within mainstream school, and despite severe language impairment, his communicative, social and work habits dramatically improved. Jeffrey had become 100% intelligible to uninitiated listeners when using practiced speech material and he was able to give basic messages to non-teaching staff. His poor speech patterns were being self-corrected during A.R.R.O.W. practice. By discrimination alone, without face reading, Jeffrey identified simple active, declarative sentences, questions or commands at 12 feet and even birdsong at 10-12 feet. He was able to follow a simple telephone conversation. By this time the auditory trainer settings had been lowered an overall 20 dB. Jeffrey was also beginning to acquire language from non-A.R.R.O.W. situations within the environment.

Now in adulthood, Jeffery is able to communicate with others from the community and was the first cochlear implant adult to receive intense A.R.R.O.W. Self-Voice therapy, whilst adjusting to his new device.

Growing Interest
After a few weeks of A.R.R.O.W. training it became clear that memory, literacy and language skills, of the Hearing Impaired Pupils were improving markedly. Clinical observations encouraged various groups of Teachers of Special Needs children to visit the Unit to see A.R.R.O.W. in operation. Travellers' children and those with Moderate and Severe Learning Problems tried the system during the visits and showed that it held considerable benefits for them. The widening of the potential population led to the establishment of a research project under the auspices of The School of Education Exeter University, supported by Birmingham University. The project looked at 'The Improvement of Listening

and Speech skills with Language Disordered Children'. (Lane 1980).

Chapter 1 - Conclusion

The need for improving literacy and communication skills of millions of people is noted. A.R.R.O.W. is defined as a multi-sensory teaching/learning system based upon the use of the Self-Voice. Reactions of children upon first meeting the recorded Self-Voice are those showing high interest despite a lack of use within education. The A.R.R.O.W. technique was first designed by the author in order to help Hearing Impaired Children improve their Speech/Language Skills. A.R.R.O.W. was initially funded through local societies and required special two track recording equipment and headphones in order to follow the approach. Pre A.R.R.O.W. communication improvement strategies were teacher directed and required a conscious effort from both teacher and pupil in order to improve speech, language and listening performances. Negative attitudes towards the use of the Self-Voice were adopted by some educators. Parents and children meeting A.R.R.O.W. were however, enthusiastic about the effects of the approach. The rationale for A.R.R.O.W. was based upon the assumption that a student would recognise their replayed errors when trying to improve their speech or language skills through a process of copying and evaluating their performance against that of the tutor. Most positive responses to the replayed Self-Voice became apparent, as was the evidence from silent lip movement, that neural processes were being involved in the overall Self-Voice replay process. Two innovative techniques, viz Echoing - the rapid replay of the student's recorded voice and Split Record - the fusion of two independent recordings into one single entity sample of speech, proved invaluable tools which are still in operation today. Two examples taken from clinical practice showed the efficacy of both techniques and their links with neurological and psychological modalities. The speed of A.R.R.O.W. is such that it allows the use of heavy repetition within a single 60 second session and additional benefits include the facility for pupils to practise alone when attempting to improve their utterances. Speech/Language 1:1 lessons utilised A.R.R.O.W. Self-Voice as part of the overall session which would also include the use of visual support material, together with well proven tactile teaching methods. A comparison between established speech improvement procedures and A.R.R.O.W. revealed the Self-Voice approach gave more positive reinforcement of a child's good utterances than a traditional 1:1 set of procedures. Early A.R.R.O.W. materials included an illustrated book and tapes of statements and questions linked to pre-recorded materials including spellings and poems. Cine-projector and speech display apparatus were also used with A.R.R.O.W. The advantages of using the approach meant that pupils could work in groups in a structured inclusion system, and consequently specialist staff costs were reduced. A Case Study of a Severely Hearing Impaired pupil revealed the benefits from using A.R.R.O.W. Self-Voice. Widening interest in the approach grew amongst educators and it was decided to initiate a research project under the auspices of Exeter and Birmingham Universities investigating the improvement of speech and listening skills.

Chapter 2
Early Listening and Speech Research

The Research Design 22

Training 22

The Test Battery 22

The Listening Range 23

Comfortable Listening Level 23

Quiet Listening Level 23

Correct/Incorrect Response Procedures 23

Environment Sound Test 24

Consonant Discrimination Test 25

Sentence Understanding Test 25

The Digit Recall Test 26

Word Recall Test 26

The Vocalisation Test 27
      The Vocalisation Test - Action of Story 27

Evidence Regarding the Listening Range 28

Listening Range Summary of Findings 28

Chapter 2 Conclusion 29

Chapter 2
Early Listening and Speech Research

Following the success of A.R.R.O.W. in the author's Hearing Impaired Unit, and interest from other specialist teachers, it was decided to initiate a Somerset research project with students experiencing speech/language disorders. The aim of the project was to investigate whether specific language skills could be improved through A.R.R.O.W. training. Students involved in the project included those with Moderate or Severe Learning Problems, in addition to those with Hearing Impairment. New stringent testing techniques, training methods and materials were required for the research. The innovative A.R.R.O.W. Self-Voice project, 'The Improvement of Speech and Listening Skills with Language Disordered Children' (Ibid), was conducted under the auspices of Exeter and Birmingham Universities. It is most rewarding that several decades later, the initiative continues to positively influence on-going A.R.R.O.W. work, not only with children, but with adults experiencing a range of literacy, speech and communication problems.

The Research Design
Two Special Schools and three Hearing Impaired Units attached to mainstream schools provided the 23 randomly selected students. Seven of these pupils attended a school for children with Moderate Learning problems, five pupils attended a school for children with Severe Learning problems and eleven pupils attended one of three Hearing Impaired Units attached to mainstream schools. Only pupils who had not previously met A.R.R.O.W., were included within the project. The basic format was an ABC design, in which each child was to be his or her own control over two consecutive 5 week periods, A-B and B-C. Normal progress was to be judged against the first 5 week A-B period, whilst the effects of A.R.R.O.W. intervention would be judged over the second 5 week B-C period. Due to time and economic constraints it was not possible to pursue the retention of any improvements or indeed fall off in performance beyond the original A,B,C design.

Training
Each child received up to 20 minutes per day A.R.R.O.W. training. All staff involved in the project were shown how to operate the system prior to the B-C intervention period. Training was delivered by Teachers of the Deaf, Specialist Teachers and Teaching Assistants. Material used for training included the commercial pre-recorded A.R.R.O.W. book and tapes, Christmas carols, and short poems or rhyming phrases designed by the author, e.g. "Cat, cat on the mat", "Dog, dog jumps the log", "Sheep, sheep, fast asleep".

The Test Battery
A battery of listening and speech tests was given at the commencement of an A-B non-A.R.R.O.W. 5 week period, which measured the effectiveness of

existent teaching provision. During this non-A.R.R.O.W. control period, teachers and assistants were asked to maintain their normal teaching strategies. After the first 5 weeks, a mid-point assessment was made at point B using the identical test battery. A.R.R.O.W. intervention took place during the second 5 week period, B-C. At the close of the B-C intervention period, the tests were administered again at Point C. In an effort to minimise any learning effect from the test-retest format of assessment, students were never informed of the accuracy of any response they made. It was intended that the listening and speech tests from within the battery would be universally applied to the entire population accepting that:

- The innate ability of each child would vary
- Verbal comprehension levels for the pupils would extend from one year old level to a ceiling of six years
- Hearing levels would range from normal to severely/profoundly deaf
- Vocal performances would range from reticent talkers with normal hearing, to severely deaf children with a positive oral attitude
- It was anticipated that articulation abilities of the children would differ

The Listening Range
The study was expected to reveal whether any differences existed between the levels of amplitude at which the various cohorts of students could discriminate speech – The Listening Range. The Listening Range of the students was judged to be the interval between two identifiable points. The first was an initial starting point in terms of volume, termed the Comfortable Listening Level. The second was a lower amplitude point at which speech was not consistently understandable and was termed the Quiet Listening Level. A tuning signal was used to standardize the sound level of recordings at the commencement of testing.

Comfortable Listening Level
The Comfortable Listening Level was the starting point for testing and was set at 65 dB, a level of intensity normally associated with conversational speech. The Hearing Impaired children had a higher Comfortable Listening Level based upon their own preferential sound settings.

Quiet Listening Level
The Quiet Listening Level was an amplitude level below that of Comfortable Listening Level and was a level at which speech was heard but was not always intelligible to the listener. Evidence from the tests showed that some mainstream pupils used in a Listening Range Pilot Project could make effective identification of numerous test sentences at 5 dB. Other pupils however, from the selected Special Needs sites, could only make effective identification some 55-60 dB above this level.

Correct/Incorrect Response Procedures
The following procedures were adopted throughout the initial testing:

1. If a child scored two consecutive correct responses at the initial Comfortable Listening Level, the amplitude was lowered 5 decibels. It was again lowered a further 5 decibels each time two or more correct responses were given. If a child gave three incorrect responses in succession, the amplitude was raised 5 decibels for the next listening task. A test was abandoned if a child achieved six consecutive failures at the Comfortable Listening Level.
2. After each five-week period the tests were repeated in the original order of presentation and at the identical amplification levels.
3. If a child exceeded the previous number of responses inside the overall time, they were allowed to continue. If the student failed to reach the original number of responses the test was discontinued at the end of the allocated time.
4. It is again stressed, that at no point was a student informed of the accuracy of the response given.

The Environment Sound Test was devised by the author and established a child's ability to identify non-verbal sounds. It was expected that this test would show whether A.R.R.O.W. speech and listening training using verbal communication skills, would influence performance in non-verbal listening tasks. Fifteen non-verbal sounds were selected from a home/school environment. Each sound was played for ten seconds maximum duration. As each sound was being played, four from fifteen black-and-white pictures, including the target picture were shown. All children were familiarised with the pictures prior to testing. Upon hearing each sound the child was required to point to the appropriate target picture. The order of sound presentation was as follows:

1. tap running
2. door opening
3. sneeze
4. footsteps
5. television
6. piano
7. children playing
8. scratching fingers
9. clapping
10. crayoning
11. motor car
12. dinner plates
13. teacher talking
14. keys jangling
15. school whistle

Environment Sound Test
See appendix 1
Investigation of pre and post A.R.R.O.W. scores, showed that whilst little progress was made during the five week 'control' period, there was an average 34% progression after the 5 week A.R.R.O.W. period. It was noted at the time, that over half of the most common errors occurred at the Comfortable Listening Level, i.e. before any marked reduction in intensity. The 50% error rate at a Comfortable Listening Level apparently suggests that the identification failure was perceptual in origin. A.R.R.O.W. intervention however, did not include training with

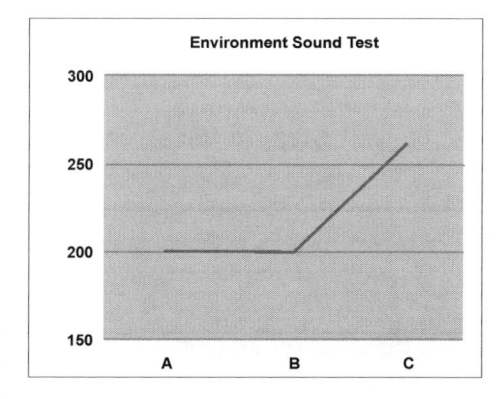

environmental sounds. This suggested to the author that a listening, rather than perceptual, deficit caused the initial A-B failures and that heightened attention skills resulted in better identification of environment sounds.

Consonant Discrimination Test
See appendix 2
The Consonant Discrimination Test, (Reed 1970), was produced under the auspices of the Royal National Institute for the Deaf and was initially designed as an early Diagnostic Hearing test. The test required students to discriminate various consonants which used a common vowel. In the A.R.R.O.W. version of the test, the child listened to a word spoken on tape and identified one from a selection of 4 pictures, each containing the same vowel but different consonants, e.g. 'jug', 'cup', 'mug', 'duck', 'owl', 'house', 'cow', 'mouse'. A total of 32 selections were required to complete the test and all pupils had been familiarised with the material prior to testing. The eight core vowel phonemes used were, mouse, cup, egg, cap, key, dog, fish, kite. The consonants used in the test were, b, d, f, g, h, j, k, l, m, n, p, r, s, t. During testing, amplification was lowered from a Comfortable Listening level to a Quiet Listening Level.

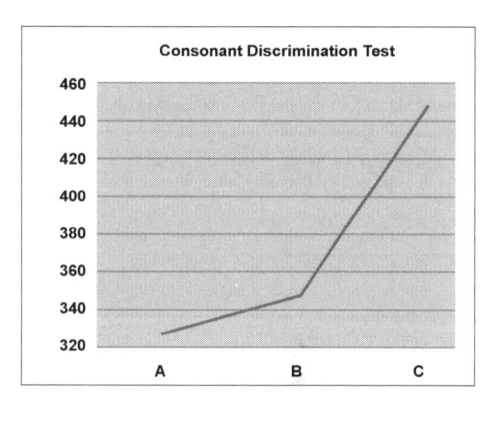

It can be seen from the graph and table in the appendix, that little progress in consonant discrimination was made in the non-A.R.R.O.W. control period. A marked shift, averaging 30% nevertheless becomes apparent after A.R.R.O.W. At no point during A.R.R.O.W training was the work centred upon consonant discrimination tasks yet results showed that the speech, language and communication skills inherent in the A.R.R.O.W Self-Voice approach, in some way improved this specific area of linguistic processing. The importance of increased attention skills (British Society of Audiology 2011) is suggested as a major factor for this improvement.

Sentence Understanding Test
See appendix 3
A Sentence Understanding Test, designed by Reynell, (1969) was administered, which required three methods of response. The first response was to point to a selection of objects when following questions or instructions. The second response was to manipulate objects to show understanding and the third was to speak to the examiner when answering questions. It was anticipated

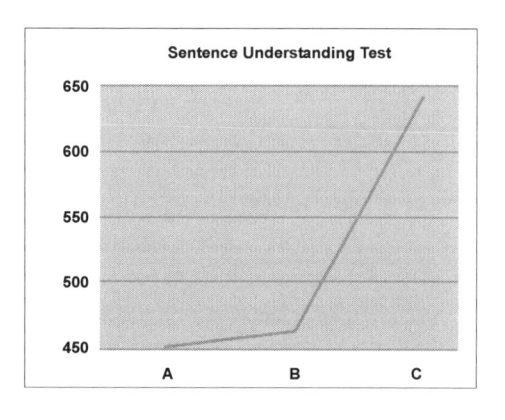

that whilst some of the children would be above the language ceiling for the Sentence Understanding Test they could still reveal movement for sentence understanding within the increasingly difficult Listening Range viz. Comfortable to Quiet Listening Levels.

A pattern again emerges in which the use of the A.R.R.O.W. Self-Voice, proves superior to other strategies used in the A-B control period. During A.R.R.O.W. intervention, no specific training was undertaken which required a student to follow the response patterns used during the Sentence Understanding Tests. The results nevertheless show an average 36.8% improvement in the ability to show understanding through either pointing, moving objects or answering questions, whereas in the five week non-A.R.R.O.W. control period, no such improvements were realised. Again, a listening skill improvement is suggested as a possible major factor for this improvement.

The Digit Recall Test
See appendix 4

This test relates to the recall of digits in increasingly longer sequences and emanated from McCarthy and Kirk, (1961). The Digit Recall Test measured a child's ability to repeat a series of numbers spoken by the examiner at a uniform rate of two per second. This test was delivered at the Comfortable Listening Level and face reading was allowed in order to minimise confusion between the similar sounding digits 5 and 9.

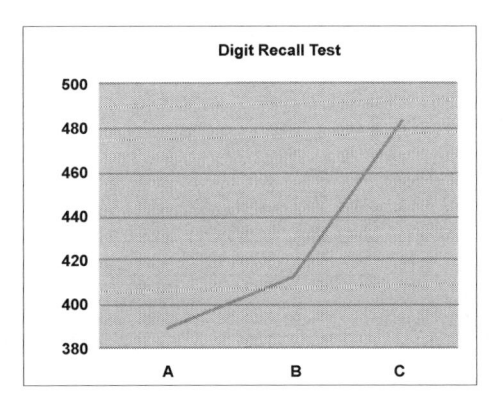

The results show that A.R.R.O.W. training improved the Working Short Term Memory of pupils by an average of 16.94%, whereas only a minimal improvement was observed during the non-A.R.R.O.W. control period. It is important to note that no specific memory training involving tasks such as repeating lists of numbers/words, or memory based games were undertaken during the A.R.R.O.W. intervention period.

Word Recall Test
See appendix 5

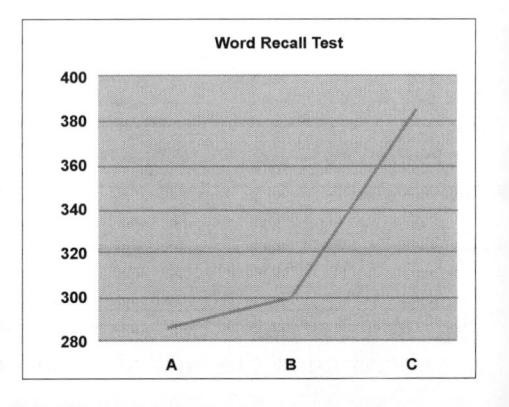

The Word Recall Test was designed by the author and followed the format of the Digit Recall Test but substituted nine words for digits. The test required a child to hold a series of words in the short term auditory memory and recall these in correct sequence. Errors of syntax were eliminated by presenting the task as a single word, rather than sentence recall format. The nine words were known by all pupils in the study – 'boat', 'tree', 'house', 'car', 'cat', 'boy', 'flower', 'girl', 'ball'. The test was delivered by the examiner at the Comfortable Listening Level and face reading was allowed in order to minimise confusion between similar sounding words.

Following A.R.R.O.W. Self-Voice intervention, results showed a marked improvement of 29% in word recall, compared to the 5 week control period, despite there being no specific word recall tasks during training. The Short Term Memory improvements were replicated many years later when A.R.R.O.W. was delivered to groups of adults with learning and/or communication problems.

The Vocalisation Test
See appendix 6

The Vocalisation Test was designed by the author to measure the number of utterances made by each pupil during the action of a story. Small dolls or models were used, these included a lady, a baby, a man, a model car and stand-up silhouettes of two houses. The examiner moved the dolls and models to help form a story which the child was asked to recount during the performance. The test was limited to one minute running time and was tape-recorded for later analysis.

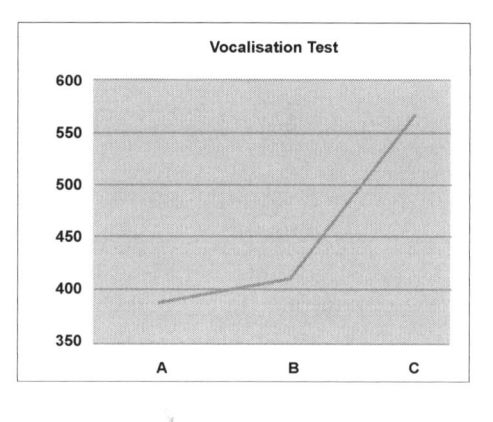

It was anticipated, that the test would encourage an oral response from all pupils irrespective of linguistic ability. The spontaneous speech samples obtained were controlled, to a certain extent, by the action which was replicated on each occasion of testing. It was felt that a vocalisation count, reflected an area of expressive language relatively free from linguistic constraints and which most approximated towards the child's attitude and ability to speak whilst following a story.

The Vocalisation Test - Action of Story
A man walks from his house to his car. He drives off in the car. A baby crawls from the side of another house and sits down in the road. The car stops in front of the baby. A lady runs from the baby's house. She picks up the baby and takes him back. The car starts again and returns home. The man gets out of the car and walks back to his house.

Each action sequence was allocated no more than five seconds. Word repetitions were counted as separate vocalisations.

The evidence gained during the A.R.R.O.W. intervention period, shows the technique averaged over 38% improvement in each pupil's ability to vocalise as the action unfolded, but there was little improvement in the 5 week control period preceding the A.R.R.O.W. intervention.

Evidence Regarding the Listening Range
It was hoped that data from the research would show evidence of the relative listening skills of a wide ability range of students, notably:

- Those with Moderate Learning Problems.
- Those with Severe Learning Problems.
- Those with Hearing Problems.

A fourth group of students were included in the Listening Range findings. These students were ten opportunity-sample mainstream children, who had been involved in a pilot study used when designing the testing procedures.

It is re-iterated that listening range was calculated as a level from a Comfortable Listening Level, based upon normal conversational speech amplitude, to a Quiet Listening Level. The Quiet Listening Level was recognised as the point at which speech is heard but is not consistently intelligible to the listener, i.e. some speech is identified correctly, some is not. Evidence for the listening range findings were taken from the three audiometric test measures which had been presented identically to all four groups. The three measures used were the Environment Sound Test, the Consonant Discrimination Test, and the Sentence Understanding Test. It was observed that Test reliability figures were extremely high for all audiometric based measures.

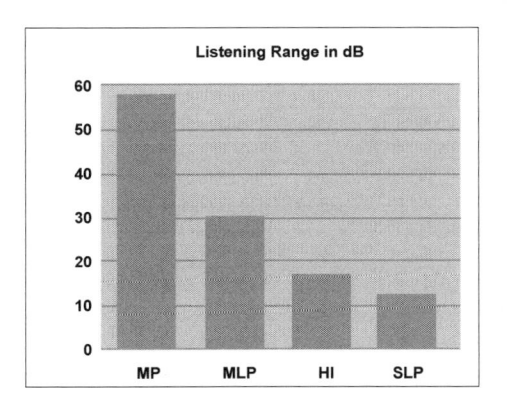

The combined Listening Range averages are listed below.

Mainstream Pupils	n = 10	Mean Listening Range 57.0 dB
Moderate Learning Problems	n = 7	Mean Listening Range 31.0 dB
		54.4% level of Mainstream Pupils' range
Hearing Impaired	n = 11	Mean Listening Range 17.6 dB
		30.8% level of Mainstream Pupils' range
Severe Learning Problems	n = 5	Mean Listening Range 13.6 dB
		23.8% level of Mainstream Pupils' range

Listening Range Summary of Findings
It is most illuminating to use the mainstream childrens' data as a norm and consider each group. Using the testing procedures as a baseline, the Moderate Learning Problem pupils were the best achievers among the two Learning Problem groups. However, their mean listening range (31.0 dB) fell well below the standard of the Mainstream Pupils' group (57 dB). Those pupils with Severe Learning Problems fell even further below the Mainstream Group in terms of the extent of their Listening Range (13.6 dB). The Hearing Impaired group were

heavily handicapped in terms of Listening Range performance (17.6 dB) compared to the mainstream group. Findings showed:

- The Hearing Impaired children used in the project operated with a Listening Range at or below the level of those with Moderate Learning Problems and sometimes near or below the level of those with Severe Learning Problems.
- Those with Severe Learning Problems were heavily impaired in terms of Listening Range performance compared to mainstream children and could virtually be regarded as Hearing Impaired with reference to movement between Comfortable and Quiet listening levels.

The Listening Range results show that children with Moderate or Severe Learning Problems could not sustain auditory attention at the same level as non-learning problem students once the sound/signal ratio lessened. As anticipated, Hearing Impaired children also had a far smaller listening range than their hearing peers. Both Learning Problem groups and the Hearing Impaired group would benefit greatly from attending schools where quiet listening conditions prevail and classrooms are equipped with the latest noise reduction speaker systems. It is interesting, that the Listening Range findings from 1979, pre-empted research conducted some thirty years later by both the Royal National Institute for the Deaf (RNID) and North West University USA, in which it is suggested that 20% students in schools/colleges do not listen as attentively as their more able peers. Recent American findings amongst Hearing Impaired adults reported by Whitton et al. (2017) confirm earlier A.R.R.O.W. findings that the total population, both normally hearing and hearing impaired, is negatively affected by the presence of background noise but that the listening skill is itself trainable with a generic child/adult population (Please see Ch.10 pp 134 - 144).

Chapter 2 Conclusion

The research project design was based upon 23 randomly selected children attending 2 Special Schools for those with Severe or Moderate Learning difficulties and 3 Hearing Impaired Units. Pupils' progress was evaluated before and after a 5 week period of normal provision A-B, followed by a similar period of A.R.R.O.W. B-C. During B-C, each pupil was to receive a short daily session of A.R.R.O.W. based upon appropriate level material. A battery of Listening and Speech Tests were applied at the commencement and close of the A, B, C periods. An audiometric type test application for some of the assessments meant that it was possible to establish a listening range in terms of amplitude for each group of pupils based upon comfortable and quiet Listening Levels. During the non-A.R.R.O.W. A-B period, no test improvements were observed. Marked improvements nevertheless, became evident after A.R.R.O.W. An Environment Sound Test clearly established the advantages of A.R.R.O.W. in which the approach was seen to benefit a non-verbal skill through the use of Self-Voice training. A test involving Consonant Discrimination tasks again resulted in an upward score movement after A.R.R.O.W. The Sentence Understanding Test results were most positive whilst two working Short Term Memory Tests involving Digit and Word Recall showed the pre-eminence of A.R.R.O.W. Self-Voice. A Vocalisation Test, in which pupils were required to talk through a short story represented by the action of dolls, revealed no improvement during the control A-B period. The same presentation after A.R.R.O.W. resulted in a highly significant improvement in vocalisation skills. Evidence became available of the listening ability of the various groups of pupils. It was found that mainstream pupils could attend to Speech even when presented through headphones at a level approximating 10 dB. Moderate Learning Problem pupils however, could not satisfactorily attend to speech unless it was presented at 34 dB. Hearing Impaired pupils could not adequately understand the test material unless it was presented at an average of 49 dB, whilst pupils with Severe Learning Problems required amplitude of some 52 dB in order to differentiate the material. The research clearly established that auditory problems exist for students with learning difficulties as well as for those with hearing impairment. The work anticipated by almost 30 years, later UK and USA research conducted into listening skills of school age students in which it has been found that children with poor listening skills are at risk of experiencing low standards of literacy. It is deemed significant that 30 years after the 1980 research was completed, adults in South West England with speech, listening and communication problems are undertook A.R.R.O.W. training for some 10 hours spread across five weeks. They too, showed parallel improvements in listening and speech skills. The more recent A.R.R.O.W. work with adults is described later in the book and has been heavily influenced by the experiences gained during the 1978-80 research project. Recent evidence from the U.S.A. confirms the effect of background noise on listening skills and the efficacy of A.R.R.O.W. principles.

Chapter 3
Research into the Self-Voice

Self-Voice Responses – Early Findings with Children and Adults 32

1. Research Design and Influences 34
   Pilot Project – Ranking of Adult Voices and Child Voices 34
   Anchor Voice 34
   Test Material 35
   Hearing Impaired Voices 35

2. Children's Appraisal of the Self-Voice 36
   High Voice Self-Esteem 36
   Low Voice Self-Esteem 36
   Hearing Impaired Children 36
   Irrevocable Finding 36

3. Possible Reasons for Positive Self-Voice Appraisal 37
   a) The Relationship Between Familiar and Liking 37
   b) The Relationship between Similarity and Liking 37
   c) The Self as Model 37

4. Effects of Using the Self-Voice 37

5. Self-Voice Recognition – A Sentence 38
   Self-Voice Recognition – A Word List (Reverse Sentence) 38
   Self-Voice Recognition - Vowel 39

6. Self-Voice Recognition Air-Bone Conduction 39

7. Echoing – a Justification 39

8. Pitch Range 39

9. Voice Self–Esteem 40

10. Voice Self-Esteem and Links to General Self-Esteem 40

Chapter 3 Conclusion 41

Chapter 3
Research into the Self-Voice

Following the success of the initial A.R.R.O.W. project, it was decided to investigate under stringent conditions, what was felt to be the central component of A.R.R.O.W, notably the student's own recorded voice, the Self-Voice. The study was a large one. Over 1000 children were involved across a five year period commencing in 1981 and ending in 1986, (Lane, 1986).

Fascinating evidence emerged of the importance of the Self-Voice during a search of the literature at the time and from the author's clinical experiences.

Self-Voice Responses – Early Findings with Children and Adults
Copeland (1960), experimented with Self-Voice feedback as a stimulus for increasing vocal utterances among Severe Learning Problem students aged between seven and sixteen years. Subjects were placed in a soundproof room and observed for five minutes. Later, the students had their own vocalisations played back to them allowing a one second delay between each utterance and voice feedback. It was noted in the Copeland experiment that all subjects increased vocalisation during Self-Voice replay. This feature is regularly noticed during A.R.R.O.W. work and was initially validated in the 1980 A.R.R.O.W. study when pupils increased the number of vocalisations by 38.87% during a 5 week period of A.R.R.O.W. training.

Waldon (1964), looked at a 6 month old child's reaction to sound. A tape recording was made of a child crying. The recording was passed through various filter bands and replayed to the child at different frequencies. The child's responses to the replayed Self-Voice were compared to responses made when listening to different frequency pure tone sounds. The experimenter concluded that the child gave more positive responses to Self-Voice sounds than from using more conventional pure tone testing.

Rousey and Holzman (Ibid), investigated adults' ability to recognize their own recorded voice from amongst 20 others. They found that 46% of the adults could recognize their voice even after a 5 minute delay.

In 1976-77, the author helped with experimental work for Bristol University on the development of a new hearing aid. He noted the importance of the Self-Voice to a severely-deaf boy when he was given a speech sound discrimination test. The boy was required to make 150 responses centred upon 13 different phonemes. The phonemes were tape-recorded onto A.R.R.O.W. equipment, firstly by the teacher, secondly by the child. The severely deaf boy was required to repeat the phonemes when listening to either his own, or the examiner's, sets of recordings. Results showed that the student achieved 74.5% correct identifications when listening to his own speech samples compared to 62%

when listening to the better articulated words of the tester. The reports support the clinical observations made at the time, whereby hearing-impaired children identified and apparently benefited more when listening to their own sometimes mis-produced recorded voices rather than an adult voice.

In the 1980s, the author experimented with voice playback with a 3 month old baby, Michael Edmonds. Michael made vocalisations which were recorded and played back to him through speakers positioned several metres away both behind him and at his side. On hearing his vocalisations, Michael turned toward the sound source and vocalised again. This response pattern was followed a second time when Michael once more heard his original recording.

Martin and Clarke (1982), used 40 infants in an experiment in which they observed the responses of day-old infants to their own recorded cries and those of other infants' cries. Crying infants who were exposed to their own recorded cry almost completely stopped crying, whilst crying infants who heard another infant's cry continued to cry. It was clear that one day old infants were differentiating their own versus other infants' cries.

In 1985, the author worked with a blind, severely-learning disabled adult whose only vocalisations were a rhythmic hum. When the Self-Voice humming vocalisations were replayed to him the adult ceased humming but recommenced after some 10-20 seconds of silence. After again replaying the Self-Voice humming, the adult once more stopped and seemingly attended to the non-humming period of silence. This effect was repeated on a second and final visit.

Virtually all educators closely involved in A.R.R.O.W. intuitively felt that the Self-Voice was the crucial element within the overall Auditory-Read-Respond-Oral-Write process. A research project was therefore, initiated into the nature of the Self-Voice, (Lane 1986). It was found that virtually no evidence from other research was available relating to several important issues. The most relevant of these issues were firstly, whether the Self-Voice was actually liked by school-age students and secondly, was the Self-Voice recognised by them. Two other points of interest were included within the study. One investigated the role of pitch in Self-Voice recognition and another considered whether there was any relationship between Voice Self-Esteem and General Self-Esteem. In order to simplify the overall debate, the four considerations will be discussed under the following headings:

1. Research Design and Influences.
2. Childrens' appraisals of the Self-Voice.
3. Possible reasons for and positive/negative Self-Voice appraisals.
4. Effects of using the Self-Voice.
5. Self-Voice Recognition – sentence, word list, vowel.
6. Self-Voice Recognition Air- Bone conduction.
7. Echoing – a justification.

8. Pitch Range.
9. Voice Self-Esteem.
10. Voice Self-Esteem and links to General Self-Esteem.

1. Research Design and Influences

Two groups of 108 children attending a mainstream Middle School in Somerset, were selected for the Self-Voice recognition and Self-Voice appraisal experiments. A third group was introduced, which consisted of 19 Hearing Impaired Children from the author's unit. One mainstream group contained pupils shown to have high Voice Self-Esteem, (High VSE), the second group contained children shown to have low Voice Self-Esteem, (Low VSE). It was hoped that by investigating the groups, evidence would be forthcoming to show whether Voice Self-Esteem was based upon either a) the child's self-evaluation of the quality of his/her Self-Voice when listening to it, or b) on other factors including how the child perceived other 'significant' people, including parents, friends and teachers, reacted to their voice rather than their own self-evaluation of its 'true' quality.

The decision was taken by the experimenter not to inform the students that they were hearing their own voices, but to require them to rank and identify their own voices amongst a series of childrens' voices of the same age and mixed gender.

Pilot Project – Ranking of Adult Voices and Child Voices

An opportunity sample of adults' and childrens' voices was presented through headsets to mainstream children of 9-13 years. The children were asked to point to the appropriate five point scale ranking number, linked to the phrase 'I see the blue car'.

5. Like a lot	4. Like	3. Neither like nor dislike	2. Dislike	1. Dislike a lot

It was found that the children in the pilot project ranked the adult voices extremely low, between 2 'Dislike' and 1 'Dislike a lot'. The adult voices were a sample taken from teachers in a neighbouring Middle School and immediately questioned several assumptions as to the use of an adult voice as a model for improving the speech and communication skills of children.

The pilot project children did not rank the child voices in the sample so negatively as they ranked the adult voices. The decision was therefore taken only to include a sample of child peer group voices in the voice assessment process. In effect, the children with Low or High Voice Self Esteem used in the experiment, would be listening to their own voice from amongst a sample of 10 other child voices.

Anchor Voice

An anchor voice was used before each voice was played to a student. The aim of the anchor voice was to standardise the decision making process as far as possible. It was felt that any preceding voice could influence the ranking of the following voice due to be heard. i.e. a disliked voice would influence the decision making when compared to the next voice heard. The anchor voice was a child selected from the mainstream school and was found to be ranked 3, 'neither like nor dislike'. Children were free to grade the anchor voice as they liked, but each child was informed how they had originally graded it. They then of course, had a baseline from which to judge other children's voices.

Test Material
Three samples of speech were used for testing which operated at varying linguistic levels.

1. A sentence, "I see the blue car," This was delivered in a continuous breath flow.

2. A list of words, 'car', 'blue', 'the', 'see', 'I'. The sentence spoken in reverse order.
The word list minimised the effects of rhythm, stress and intonation.

3. A single front vowel 'i'
This utterance contained no linguistic cues.

Ten voices were used on the tape. All voices gave the same sample of speech, with the anchor voice intervening before each new sample was played. Before assessment the children recorded the three samples themselves on track two of a multi track recorder. During the testing, track one was used to play the ten voices, track two contained the child's Self-Voice. Switching between tracks was effected quietly. The children were not informed that their voices would be played or indeed given any clues that their voices were being replayed from amongst the sample voices. The position of the child's Self-Voice within the sample varied according to the utterance.

Hearing Impaired Voices
Recordings included those taken from three Hearing Impaired children who were receiving speech therapy. In this way, it was hoped to establish the liking/disliking of Hearing Impaired voices by mainstream children and also by Hearing Impaired children themselves.

2. Children's Appraisal of the Self-Voice

The author had found that there was a commonly held belief amongst many teachers that the Self-Voice was disliked and there was, therefore, little point in playing back to a child their own voice. Investigation of the data however, showed this belief to be erroneous.

High Voice Self-Esteem

A ranking dominance for the Self-Voice (SV) occurred with the High VSE group across all three forms of utterance, Sentence, Word List and Vowel.

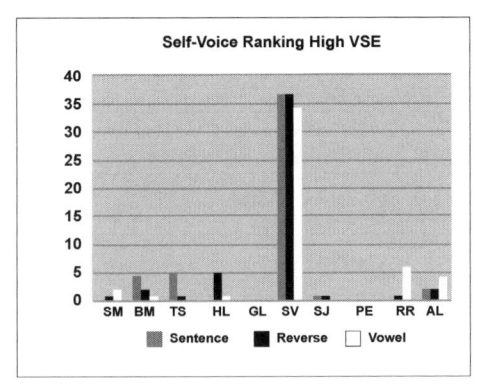

Low Voice Self-Esteem

Low VSE pupils ranked the Self-Voice higher significantly more often, than any other voice for all forms of utterance. It was most interesting that children who ostensibly disliked their own voices according to pencil and paper tests, nevertheless rated them higher than any other voice when they were actually played to them, despite being totally unaware that their own voice was being presented.

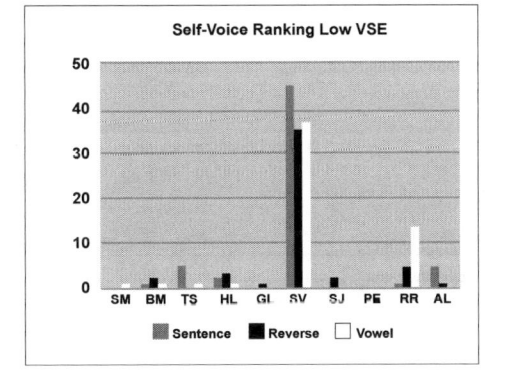

Hearing Impaired Children

Hearing Impaired children, save for the vowel condition, followed the Normally Hearing children and ranked their own voices highest and the three Hearing Impaired voices used in the recordings lowest. Seven from the 19 Hearing Impaired children were receiving speech therapy because of various speech deficiencies, yet still ranked their own voices higher than any other.

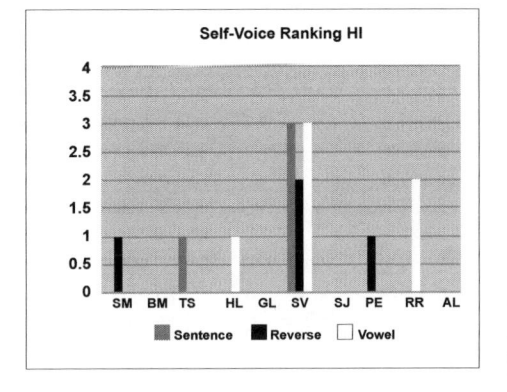

Irrevocable Finding

If the totals for the groups are combined, the Self-Voice was ranked highest on 108 occasions whilst the next most popular voice was ranked highest on only 8 occasions. i.e. the Self-Voice achieved more than 13x highest ranking than the next most popular voice. All groups of children, those with High VSE, those with low VSE and the Hearing Impaired, ranked their own voices higher than others. Investigation of the scores showed that those students who had not recognised their voices in the Self-Voice Recognition Test, nevertheless ranked their own voices highest on the Self-Voice appraisal test measure i.e. it was a liking of the Self-Voice 'per se' rather than ranking it higher because it was recognised as 'me'. If it had been recognised as 'me' when ranking the voice, the low VSE children would presumably have given themselves a low score, this in fact did not occur.

3. Possible Reasons for Positive Self-Voice Appraisal
It is suggested that the following factors may have influenced the positive Self-Voice rankings made by students.

a) The Relationship Between Familiar and Liking
The familiar-liking argument suggests that the more familiar an item, the better the chance of it being liked. The Self-Voice is one of the voices most heard by each person in daily life and is possibly, for many people, the most commonly heard voice. Exposure to the Self-Voice therefore, leads to some form of conscious subliminal familiarity which follows the familiar-liking pattern. This view is apparently justified by the evidence presented within the study.

b) The Relationship between Similarity and Liking
Another idea for consideration, suggests that the more similar one item is to another, the greater the chance of it being liked. The speaker's replayed voice, being an echo of his/her own utterance, is therefore most similar to the original vocalisation and will be regarded favourably. Results from this study would seem to confirm this theory insofar as the Self-Voice was ranked highest by children irrespective of Voice Self-Esteem, age, gender or academic ability.

c) The Self as Model
It is felt that using oneself as a model can help lessen academic failure and that the self-as-model principle inherent within the A.R.R.O.W. Self-Voice approach, helps the pupil acquire a perfectly mastered pattern of reading behaviour.

4. Effects of Using the Self-Voice
A 14 year old female student at a Taunton College offered comments upon using the Self-Voice which fully support the 'familiar – liking', 'similar – liking' and 'self-as-model' discussions. After using Split Recording and Self-Voice playback of sentences taken from a passage, the teenager was immediately observed to improve her reading fluency. Two difficult-to-read sections were practised and recorded in parts before being replayed as a fluent utterance. On the first occasion of hearing herself, the teenager's lips moved in synchronisation with her replayed voice. After listening to herself on replay, she was able to read the passage in a much improved fashion. She reported that she was not aware her lips were moving during the first replay of her own voice. She states:

"I listened to it because it was my own voice and I liked to hear what my own voice sounded like. I've not listened to my own voice much. I liked it, I found it very cool."

5. Self-Voice Recognition – A Sentence
See appendix 7
In the Self-Voice Research study, students were required to identify the Self-Voice from a sample of nine peer group voices. It will be remembered that each voice spoke a sentence, list of words, or vowel. The Self-Voice was recorded by each student and placed amongst the other sample voices. The Self-Voice recording was replayed three times. Firstly immediately after recording i.e. within 1-2 seconds, secondly, following another voice, a delay of 11-15 seconds, and thirdly, following eleven other voices which resulted in a 2-3 minute delay from the original recording.

Students listened to the voices through headsets and pointed to a card worded Me/Not Me.

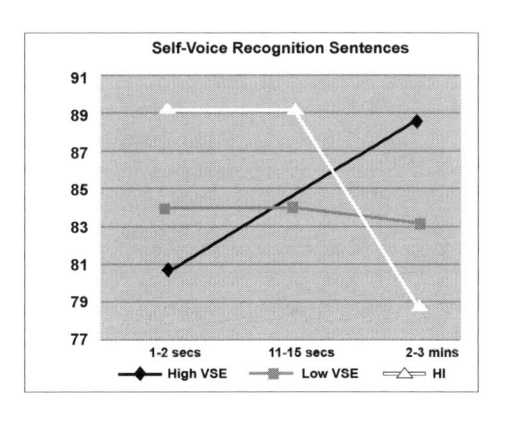

The groups were split into High Voice Self Esteem, Low Voice Self-Esteem and Hearing Impaired.

It can be seen that for Sentence Recognition the three groups achieved high Self-Voice identification in all delay conditions. Interestingly, the Hearing Impaired group were superior in two from the three Me/Not me selections, yet showed a slight fall-off for the third decision after 2-3 minutes delay.

Self-Voice Recognition – A Word List (Reverse Sentence)
See appendix 8 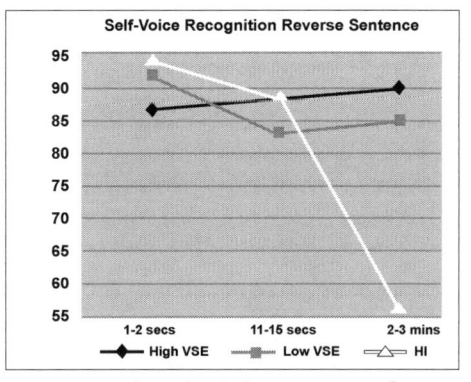
In the Reverse Sentence Condition, the Hearing Impaired group again were superior in the 2-3 sec and 11-15 delay conditions. There was however, a marked fall off in the 2-3 minute delay condition. It is suggested by the author that this falloff is probably because the suprasegmental features of speech, rhythm, stress and intonation, were reduced with the non-sentence conditions. The evidence suggests that once meaning is taken away from a speech sample, as in a reverse sentence, then the Hearing Impaired are less effective than their hearing peers after the 11-15 second storage period has passed.

Self-Voice Recognition - Vowel
See appendix 9

In the recognition tasks for the short vowel 'I', all three groups had a sharp decline in performance after an interval of 11-15 seconds i.e. immediately before the next Self-Voice recording was heard. The deterioration in performance after the initial 2-3 second presentation suggests that whilst recognition based upon voice quality alone is possible within the immediate echoic storage level i.e. 1-2 seconds, it is undoubtedly strengthened by other linguistic cues, e.g. the content of the speech utterance, in more delayed conditions of recall (See appendix 9).

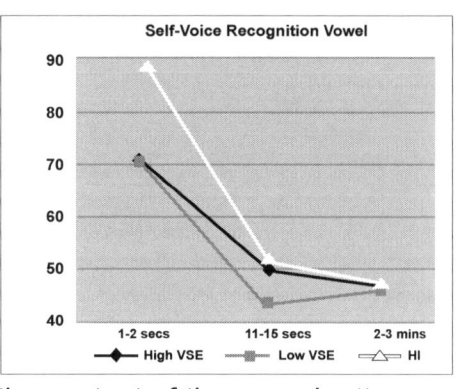

6. Self-Voice Recognition Air-Bone Conduction
Current work with pupils of school age, often reveals that pupils recognise and smile at their own voice even when recording purely by microphone and afterwards listening 'free field' to their original recording, without using headsets. In effect this indicates that the features of Self-Voice recognition and liking do not rely entirely upon bone conduction.

7. Echoing – a Justification
All groups achieved high Self-Voice recognition in the first two delay conditions. The Hearing Impaired group, however, scored lower than the other two groups in the case of the reverse sentence after a 2-3 minute delay. All groups operated at a 'chance' level after the immediate feedback condition had passed with single vowel utterances. This lower score was possibly a result of reducing the amount of rhythm, stress and intonation usually evident in normal "running speech". The evidence of the higher recognition rate after the earliest replay conditions, strongly supports the use of the Echoing technique during speech improvement work. If voice quality is an important aim with children experiencing speech problems, it seems sensible to echo back utterances within the optimum period for their retention i.e. up to 3 seconds. Any lengthier delay between utterance and replay, would presumably decrease the extent that those vocal features, inherent in voice quality, remain within acoustic storage.

8. Pitch Range
A secondary level investigation looked at the range of pitch against which the Self-Voice could be identified. Dr Duncan Grant (Bristol University) suggested the use of a vari-pitch control audio cassette system to higher or lower Self-Voice recordings. Using a vari-pitch control audio cassette system, it was possible to higher or lower Self-Voice recordings. An opportunity sample of 37 students from the project were presented with the same voice identification tasks, 'Me/Not Me', for a sentence and vowel as the pitch was being raised or

lowered. It was found that a difference of pitch tolerance existed between the Normally Hearing mainstream children and the Hearing Impaired children when identifying the limits for Self-Voice identification. Normally Hearing children would move less than 9% in either base or treble direction before confirming a "Not me" situation when hearing their own voice. Hearing Impaired children however, were prepared to have their voices shifted more than 11.5% before they moved to a "Not me" pattern, i.e. a difference of some 27% from their hearing counterparts. Close scrutiny of the Hearing Impaired scores showed that whilst some of the Hearing Impaired children had very good speech, they nevertheless allowed a far greater shift of pitch than Normally Hearing children, before stating "Not me" and in addition, could not consistently sing in tune. It was felt that the finding suggests possible reasons why they, and other, Hearing Impaired children/adults have difficulty in pitching their voice appropriately in order to hum or sing a melody. For a period of time pitch shifting for falsetto type utterances became the norm in speech improvement work with Hearing Impaired children.

9. Voice Self–Esteem
See appendix 10
Research showed that a student has a perception about the positive or negative effects his voice has upon other people, ie there is Voice Self-Esteem. Using Item analysis methods for test design, 22 self-referent statements, emanating from childrens' comments, were given to a sample of 900 children. It was shown that the children of mixed gender have well defined ideas about the effect of their voice upon others. A selection of comments, some positive, some negative, were finalised e.g. 'My friends like my voice' 'I've got the best voice in the world' 'My parents love my voice'. Some children endorsed these as being true of themselves, other children offered a negative, 'not true' response.

10. Voice Self-Esteem and Links to General Self-Esteem
As a secondary level investigation, a Global Self-Esteem measure was given to nine hundred children of mixed gender aged 9-13 years. The Global Self-Esteem measure contained 37 items relating to a home/school environment. Results, as expected, showed that children differed in their General Self-Esteem. According to the measure, some children had High Self-Esteem, some had Low Self-Esteem and some operated within an average between the two. When results from the Global Self-Esteem and Voice Self-Esteem measure were compared, it was shown that a low order, but significant correlation, existed between Voice Self-Esteem and Global Self-Esteem. It suggested that pupils with high Voice Self-Esteem were more likely to have high Global Self-Esteem, whilst pupils with low Voice Self-Esteem were likely to have low Global Self-Esteem. This has considerable implications for educators. Criticism of a student's voice is akin to a general criticism of the student, and of course assumes that a student is aware of their own speech qualities. The author's personal experiences, from now far-distant schooldays, and more recent observations of other children, suggest that the link between the Self-Voice and Global Self-Esteem should be carefully respected.

Chapter 3 Conclusion

Following the success of the listening and speech research, it was decided to investigate in greater depth the role of the Self-Voice. Early experiments and resultant findings with children and adults, together with the author's clinical observations, suggested that the replayed Self-Voice evoked a marked reaction amongst subjects listening to recordings of themselves. A research project based upon two, as then unproven major premises concerning the Self-Voice was planned. The two issues were the liking/disliking of the Self-Voice by school age students. The second was the recognition/non-recognition of the Self-Voice. Third and fourth less prominent questions, asked whether Voice Self-Esteem was a valid concept and if so did it relate to General Self-Esteem? A Voice Self-Esteem measure was devised and two groups of 108 children were selected for the project based upon whether they had High or Low Voice Self-Esteem. A third group was formed entirely of Hearing Impaired pupils. A pilot project established the disliking of adult voices by pupils and it was therefore, decided only to use children's peer group voices within the 5 point scale like/dislike voice sample. An anchor voice was integrated within the test, against which all voice evaluations would be based. Children judged ten peer voices, in addition to their own saying a sentence, word list and single vowel. The voice sample included three children with Hearing Impairment. The Self-Voice was ranked highest for all conditions by both groups of High and Low Voice Self-Esteem and Hearing Impaired Children. The findings were irrevocable. Two reasons are suggested for the pre-eminence of the Self-Voice based upon familiarity and similarity. A theory of the benefits of using Self as Model is suggested and a student's reaction to A.R.R.O.W. well supports this premise. Recognition Tests of the Self-Voice delivering a sentence, word list or vowel, across varying delay conditions, conclusively proved that High Self-Voice recognition was achieved by all groups for the Sentence, Word List and Vowel Tests. Self-Voice recognition and liking is not entirely dependant upon bone conduction. A decline in vowel recognition after immediate feedback supported the use of the echoing technique during speech improvement work. A secondary investigation established that Self-Voice recognition is pitch dependent and that Hearing Impaired Children exceeded the range of those with normal hearing. The study established that pupils have Voice Self-Esteem i.e. have perceptions of the positive/negative effects their voice has upon significant others and that Voice Self-Esteem is related to General Self-Esteem.

Chapter 4
The Self-Voice, Internal Speech and Learning Attainments

The Self-Voice and Internal Speech: Some Considerations 44

The Mental Lexicon 44

Echoic Storage of the Self-Voice 44

Interrelationship Between Literacy Skills and Internal Speech 45

Internal Speech Processes and Spelling 46

The Somerset Experiment – Phonological Coding 46

Test Procedures 47

Effects of A.R.R.O.W. upon Working Short Term Memory 47

Visual Coding – A Comment 48

Rote Learning Through Self-Voice Echo 48

Self-Voice Memory Recall Tasks 50

Internal Speech and the Self-Voice - A Running Dialogue 50

Chapter 4 Conclusion 51

Chapter 4
The Self-Voice, Internal Speech and Learning Attainments

The Self-Voice and Internal Speech: Some Considerations
The use of internalised thinking, or internal speech, is best described as talking to oneself in one's head. The three way relationship between the A.R.R.O.W. Self-Voice, the 'normal' internalised voice and the movement of the articulators, is very close indeed and is evidenced by silent lip movement during Self-Voice replay. It should be noted however, that the voice used during A.R.R.O.W. recording, is subtly different to the voice normally used for internalising our thoughts. Despite this slight difference, it is widely recognised by A.R.R.O.W. practitioners, that when recording and listening back through A.R.R.O.W. headphones, the digital match between the spoken and replayed utterance is extremely close.

The Mental Lexicon
It is suggested that words, or indeed phonemes, are actually stored in our own voice within our mental dictionary, the lexicon. The recorded Self-Voice is therefore, one which bears great similarity to any such sound pattern templates in the lexicon. It is likely that the time it takes to access the mental lexicon in memory tasks using A.R.R.O.W. Self-Voice, is substantially reduced compared to listening to another voice. This superiority is most probably because the procedure for matching any Self-Voice speech sounds, to the templates in the lexicon, is less complicated and therefore takes less time to complete, than it would for listening and processing phonemes from another voice.

Echoic Storage of the Self-Voice
In earlier chapters a seemingly innate reaction to the replayed Self-Voice was observed from the early days of A.R.R.O.W when used with school-age pupils. Later clinical observations with adults further reveal the importance of the Self-Voice as a Psychological/Neurological event.

During 2012, Edward, an adult with Head Injury, tried A.R.R.O.W. Edward had an overloud distorted voice when talking to people and agreed to repeat and listen back to four simple active declarative sentences.

A train.
A green train.
A noisy train.
An old train.

After recording these and listening on playback, he was observed to:

- unknowingly mouth each word from the sentences as they were being played to him
- smile broadly at the close of the passage
- recognise the recorded voice as his own – "me"

When asked if he knew his lips were moving when listening to his recorded voice he replied "no".

This evidence of subvocalisation had been noted with Hearing Impaired children several decades earlier. After listening to the Self-Voice, it was pointed out to Edward that he needed to speak in a softer manner. He undertook the exercise again. He responded appropriately when practising A.R.R.O.W. and additionally showed that he could easily follow and successfully repeat items after listening to his own recordings. Edward's silent mouthing again raises the question of the nature of the mental lexicon for some of those with less than perfect vocalisation skills. It would seem to the author, that some at least, of those with poor speech/language patterns, are most likely organising their vocalisations in their current, perhaps distorted, internal voice. Confirmation of this point of view came a week later, when speaking to Colin, a brain injured adult from Yeovil, who reported that he 'thought' in his current atypical voice as he could not remember the sound of his pre-injury speech.

A female non-English speaking/reading resident of Kuwait, was being shown a combination of Split Record and Echoing techniques. The Kuwaiti lady, with tutor help, recorded in two parts, "We can use/a kaleidoscope." On Echoing replay, her lips moved in synchronisation with her recording, although she could never in fact, have had any knowledge of the meaning of the sentence or the words used. It is suggested, that when her lips were seen to be moving, she was involuntarily responding to a short term echoic storage of a sound pattern linked to the articulatory loop. The lip moving response, obviously occurred before any higher level linguistic processes were employed which involved extracting meaning and subsequent rehearsal strategies.

An English teenager was given in Danish, the equivalent of, "I can play football", without seeing any text. After copying a Danish teacher's native tongue version, he recorded the short sentence in Danish and unknowingly moved his lips in synchronisation with his replayed recording. Again, the student had no knowledge of the material he had recorded. It is felt, that the phenomena once more indicated some link between a lower level form of short term echoic storage and the articulatory loop.

Interrelationship Between Literacy Skills and Internal Speech
It is well established that there is a three fold relationship between reading performance, internal speech, and subvocalisation. Subvocalisation sometimes involves the silent movement of the articulators in reading tasks, although it can be observed in non-reading situations. One of the first noticeable effects with pupils when undertaking A.R.R.O.W. in 1975 and which has persisted since, is

the involuntary movement of their lips when listening to the replayed Self-Voice. This observation still holds true today and reveals the presence of a link between the replayed Self-Voice and those internal speech processes, including subvocalisation, which are so necessary to literacy skill acquisition. It was noted in the early years that the observable movement of the articulators, when listening to the Self-Voice, differed from pupil to pupil and was not consistently evident for all pupils.

It is believed that one of the primary roles of internal speech is to allow the reader to restructure written language by adding rhythm, stress and intonation to text in order to add meaning. Amongst proficient readers, there is an increasing use of internal speech in relationship to the difficulty of the material being read. The more difficult the material, the more the use of subvocalisation. Sometimes a person will read aloud a difficult passage in order to elicit meaning. Conrad (1979) found that there was a direct correspondence between the use of internal speech and reading ability of deaf school leavers. In effect this means the more able the reader, the greater the use of subvocalisation, the less able the reader, the lesser the use of subvocalisation. It is noted that internal speech develops at different rates according to the ability of the reader with the slower reader acquiring the internalising skills later than more proficient peers.

It is most interesting that an A.R.R.O.W. trained Teacher of the Deaf reported that some of her Hearing Impaired signers would unwittingly sign to themselves when watching themselves signing on Video replay, yet did not sign to themselves when watching others (Parsons, J. 2002). This suggests that the pupils were internalising their thoughts using a sign system and that the Self-Sign was, in a pattern akin to the Self-Voice, a potent agent in their thought processes.

Internal Speech Processes and Spelling
Whilst there is evidence concerning the role of internal speech in reading ability, there was at the time of Conrad's work, far less information on the relationship between internal speech and spelling ability. It is accepted that more able spellers articulate subvocally, i.e. utilise internal speech when writing words and may also make slight hand or finger movements when orally 'spelling' a word aloud.

The Somerset Experiment – Phonological Coding
An experiment was undertaken at a Middle School in Somerset (Lane 1990). The aim of the study was to establish firstly, whether there was any relationship between the use of internal speech and spelling ability and secondly, whether the use of internal speech could be nurtured with children of school age.

The subjects were 105 children with a mean age of 9 years 5 months. The children were given an Internal Speech Test (Conrad Ibid). In essence this test indicates whether a child tries to remember a word's sound or a word's shape when undertaking recall tasks from 24 lists of words. The pupils were required to recall a series of similar sounding words 'true', 'who', 'blue', 'through', 'zoo' (rhyming words) or similarly shaped words, 'home', 'farm', 'firs', 'bean', 'lane', (four letters with a large letter leading three equal size letters). Conrad (Ibid) had shown that the similar sounding words confuse more on recall than similar shaped words having dissimilar sounds. From these and earlier experiments, Conrad had found that in memory tasks involving a series of words or letter sounds, a great proportion of subjects used an auditory, phonological code, rather than a visual code when recalling information.

Test Procedures

Lists of similarly shaped and similar sounding words were permanently displayed in each classroom used in the project. Children were familiarised with these lists prior to testing. Three cards from each list were shown in succession to the children who were then required to write down the words. Results revealed that 90 from 105 children relied upon the auditory modality when trying to recall the order of words i.e. they spoke the words and letters in their heads when trying to recall them. Fifteen out of the 105 children did not follow this internalised, phonological, auditory pattern, but tried to remember words by their shape, not by the sounds they made. The fifteen children therefore appeared to code words in a visual, rather than a phonological form. Further inspection of the class teachers' records showed, most interestingly, that 13 of these 15 children were ranked in the lowest third of the year according to spelling ability, whilst the remaining 2 from 15 were at the fringe of the poor spellers. The 15 visually dominant children with less than average spelling ability were given A.R.R.O.W. training on 20 commonly misspelt words. The words for training did not include any used in the original internal speech test. Normal 15-20 minute A.R.R.O.W. training times were followed throughout a two week period and children were supervised by A.R.R.O.W. trained volunteers or teaching assistants. After the two week training period, the Internal Speech Test was again administered. Results showed that 14 of the original 15 visually dominant children had shifted their coding strategies to the more normal phonological code and some in fact, on re-test, were seen to be silently mouthing some of the words that were being presented. The control group of 90 auditorily dominant children were found to have retained their original form of phonological processing.

Effects of A.R.R.O.W. upon Working Short Term Memory

Examination scores also revealed a marked improvement in the short term memory scores for those visually dominant children who received A.R.R.O.W. training. When effecting a shift to the auditory mode, the 15 children improved their short-term memory recall of non-rhyming words by 35%. The 1990 experimental groups means of words correctly remembered in sequence, rose from 23.69 to 32.15 from a possible 36 correct. The control Group scores however, only rose from 32.7 to 34.4. It should be again emphasised that the improvements for the experimental group were realised from the children attempting to learn spellings of commonly misspelt words using A.R.R.O.W. and were not the result of a direct attempt to shift coding practice using the test material.

It is accepted that there is a close link between the use of internal speech and memory span for auditory recall tasks. It appears that by using A.R.R.O.W. spelling techniques, primarily to help develop vocalisation-based internal speech, working short term memory was also affected in a positive fashion. The improvement of the working Short Term Memory Word List recall after A.R.R.O.W. reflects the encouraging short term memory results gained earlier with language disordered children during the 1980 A.R.R.O.W. project.

Visual Coding – A Comment

From the Internal Speech Study, it can be argued that reliance on a visual form of coding, without recourse to some form of verbalisation, is questionable in terms of childrens' spelling progress. It is however clear, that given A.R.R.O.W. training, an appropriate coding strategy can be employed by children within a short period of time. It was felt that the A.R.R.O.W. intervention children involved in the study, had not suddenly become proficient spellers, but had in fact honed their ability to use vocalising skills in order to both code and learn 'how to learn' a spelling, provided it lay within their short-term memory span.

Rote Learning Through Self-Voice Echo

A sample of 25 male students at a school for Dyslexics in the United Kingdom were selected for inclusion in a times table learning project (Lane and Chinn 1986). When tested on 159 times table facts, the 25 adolescents, who ranged in age from 14.3 to 18 years and in IQ ranged from 89 to 126, achieved an average score of 1.4 with the highest of 6 and the lowest of 0.

Using a tape player, fifteen, times-tables facts, $3 \times 9 = 27$, $4 \times 8 = 32$, etc. were presented randomly through headsets at 3 second intervals. This time limit aimed for direct recall answers only, as many Dyslexics might have computed answers in several different ways if the time allowed for an answer had been longer.

The students were grouped into 5 groups of 5, and trained for 10 minutes under tutor supervision for 5 consecutive days in 1 from 5 methods.

1. A.R.R.O.W. tape-recorder Self-Voice Echoing. The student recorded a times table factor in his own voice which was then echoed back several times within 1 or 2 seconds by an operator until the student seemed to have achieved mastery.

2. A.R.R.O.W. tape-recorded Tutor voice - the same equipment and overall techniques were used but only the Tutors voice was recorded and replayed to the student.

3. Commercial tape-recorder for Self-Voice Echoing - a small cassette recorder with built in microphone was used with earphones. The student's own voice was recorded and played back. The replay button produced a high-pitched noise which caused distraction to each student.

4. Read and say. The student read aloud the times table facts from written cards used one at a time until apparent mastery was achieved.

5. Write and say. The student wrote out the times table facts saying them as he wrote each fact down.

The students were retested using the original test procedures, one day, one week and one month after training sessions. The Specialist Teacher noted that the students using the A.R.R.O.W. Self-Voice learning technique made the greatest use of silent mouthing (subvocalising) as they practised the items to be learnt.

The total training time for each student was 50 minutes. The Specialist Teacher involved in the project observed that the gains made in this short time scale have to be assessed against many hours of instruction throughout their school career prior to using A.R.R.O.W. techniques.

It is clear from the study that the greatest improvements in multiplication table recall came from those techniques using the student's own voice and that the use of A.R.R.O.W. Self-Voice technologies proved superior to other recording systems available during the project.

A UK Speech and Language Therapist wrote of her experiences using A.R.R.O.W. and notes the advantages of Self-Voice (Crewdson 1996).
Her observations may be summarised as follows:

1. An increase in subvocalisation and rehearsal thereby supporting memory and comprehension.
2. An increase in accurate repetition of sentences of increasing length and complexity.
3. An improvement in story retelling from a series of pictures.
4. A greater ability to put words into sentences.

Self-Voice Memory Recall Tasks
See appendix 11

Jonathan Vile (1998) conducted a dichotic Self-Voice listening experiment at the University of Surrey. The aim was to discover whether listening to the Self-Voice was superior to listening to other voices in memory tasks.

Adult subjects recorded a list of words consisting of 20 single syllable animal-based nouns, 'horse', 'mouse', 'dog' etc. The recordings were then spliced to provide new recordings of two lists, each list being 10 words long. After a delay period of two weeks the adults began their listening/learning tasks. In effect, the adults were listening to two lists of words being played at the same time, one list for each ear. One ear received animal words in the Self-Voice, the other ear received animal words in another adult voice. In each case they heard 20 words in total, all of which they had spoken before. After the recordings had been played, the subjects were then asked to write down the words they had just heard.

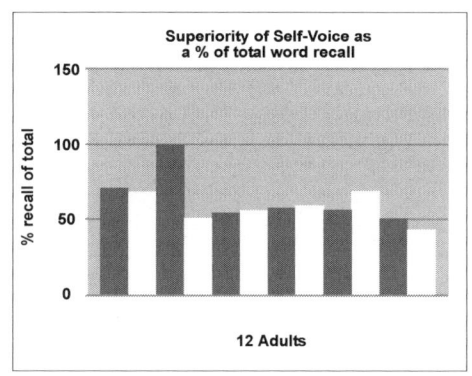

Evidence reveals that a majority of the informants remembered more of the words spoken in their own voice than those spoken in a different voice. Of the words recalled, 63% of remembered words were in the Self-Voice. Vile notes that this is a 24% bigger increase than would have been expected. He reached the conclusion that the Self-Voice effect was probably due to the aid that the Self-Voice gives to memory, due to quicker access times to the student's own Self-Voice mental lexicon.

Internal Speech and the Self-Voice - A Running Dialogue

Speech is internalised in order to help clarify thoughts and set up spoken responses to statements or questions. It is self-evident that the internalised voice, as heard in the head, sets up templates which relate closely to the voice as spoken "live" at a particular time.

The author once gave an Awareness Talk in Gloucestershire whilst having a hoarse voice as a result of a very heavy cold. When talking to the audience, he clearly appreciated that the timbre of his voice was affected by the virus. During the very close interval between listening to questions from the floor and formulating an internal answer prior to speaking this aloud, he realised that internalised, pre "live" utterances, were being formulated in his "hoarse" voice, not the voice he would normally have used. This phenomena well illustrates the matching effect of templates and the "live" Self-Voice. It also suggests an explanation for the positive impact when using a headset-boom microphone configuration which sets up a near perfect match between the spoken and replayed Self-Voice. Hearing Impaired students, of course, have an almost permanent mental lexicon template/recorded Self-Voice match, insofar as they hear both "live" speech and also their Self-Voice recordings through their hearing aids.

Chapter 4 Conclusion

The use of internalised thinking, or internal speech is described as talking to oneself in one's head. The relationship between the replayed Self-Voice and internal speech is established, as is the closeness of the match between the voice spoken through headphones and replayed Self-Voice. It is suggested that our own voice is the storage agent for speech/language material used in our mental dictionary (Mental Lexicon) and that the replayed Self-Voice thereby speeds and assists the processing of information. Examples are given showing that the replayed Self-Voice and silent lip movement interact with some form of echoic storage and that this can apparently operate independently of higher level reading and spelling learning processes. Examples are cited in which replayed Self-Voice foreign language utterances, holding no meaning for a speaker, nevertheless, induced silent lip movements. An interrelationship exists between reading, subvocalisation, (the silent movement of the articulators) and internal speech. Sub-vocalisation develops at different speeds according to the reading ability of the student, with the slower reader acquiring the skill later than a more capable peer. A Somerset based experiment investigated the use and nurturing of internal speech when using A.R.R.O.W. for the learning of spellings. An opportunity sample of 105 Year 4 pupils undertook an Internal Speech Test in which the best recall of lists of words were dependent upon the student's use of a phonological (word sound) rather than visual (word shape) form of coding. Fifteen pupils who were found to use a visual form of coding were amongst the lower achievers for spelling and were selected for a 2 hour program of A.R.R.O.W. training. The students were re-tested and were shown to have improved their working Short Term Memory skills and also moved to a more widely used form of phonological coding in terms of word recall performances. The disadvantages of solely using a visual form of coding for the learning of spellings are noted. In an experiment with Dyslexic students, the use of A.R.R.O.W. Self-Voice proved to be superior to all other methods in the learning of multiplication table facts and that listening to an adult voice was less effective than listening to the Self-Voice. A Speech and Language Therapist writes of her experiences using A.R.R.O.W. and confirms the improvement in memory based linguistic tasks involving comprehension and sentence repetition. An experiment involving word list recall by graduate students showed that recall using Self-Voice word list training was 24% superior to word list training in another adult voice. It is suggested a flexible matching of templates exists between the mental lexicon and an adult's contemporary running speech, so that a change in a speaker's voice timbre, may in fact, result in a comparable change in a speaker's mapping and use of internal speech at that particular time.

Chapter 5
The Development of A.R.R.O.W. Reading - Spelling Programs

A.R.R.O.W. Pre-Reading Skill Acquisition 55

Pre-A.R.R.O.W. School Experiences 56

Chanting 56

National Speech Standards 56

Introducing A.R.R.O.W. Reading and Spelling Programs 57

Poetry 57

Spellings 58

A.R.R.O.W. Procedures, Failure of Cascading and Need for Tutor Training . 58

The Use of a Tutor and Single A.R.R.O.W. Cassette Recorder 58

Disadvantages of the A.R.R.O.W. Audio Cassette System 59

The Emergence of Computer Technology 59

Topics 60

Topics - Non Access to Text When Recording 61

Grammatical Error Work 61

A.R.R.O.W. DVD Pre-Reader and Free Field Techniques 61

Student Centred Language 61

Alphabet 62

Spellings 62

Non-sense vowel consonant vowel words 62

High and Medium Frequency Words 63

Personal Spelling Profile System 63

High Ability Level Spellings 63

Curriculum Based Spellings – Free Field Facility 64

Spelling Rules 64

System Flexibility – Timescales used for the Application of A.R.R.O.W. 64

The Format of the Tutor Training Program 65

Trainer of Tutors Course 65

Chapter 5 Conclusion 65

Chapter 5
The Development of A.R.R.O.W. Reading-Spelling Programs

Several research projects into A.R.R.O.W. were conducted across an eight year period, 1978-86. The projects occurred during a time when the author was also developing curriculum based Topics and Spelling schemes for his Hearing Impaired Unit. The A.R.R.O.W. schemes were successfully applied to other Special Needs students attending the host mainstream school. The Hearing Impaired Unit therefore, widened its population to include students with Moderate Learning Problems, Dyslexia and Visual Impairments. It soon became clear that the use of A.R.R.O.W. could be further extended to include the improvement of literacy skills with groups of mainstream pupils outside the host school, provided appropriate reading/spelling programs could be developed.

A.R.R.O.W. Pre-Reading Skill Acquisition
Early research conducted in 1980 had shown the potential of the Self-Voice to improve various listening and speech skills including:

- Consonant Discrimination and Sentence Understanding
- Short Term Memory for Digits and Words
- Vocalisation Skills

Studies into the Self-Voice conducted with mainstream and Hearing Impaired students revealed that by using the student's own voice within A.R.R.O.W. learning tasks, several important criteria were being met:

- The student was being presented with a most favoured voice
- The student was meeting and recognising a familiar and identifiable voice
- The use of internal speech associated to phonological coding, was being encouraged
- Rote learning of required information could be improved
- The A.R.R.O.W. concept allowed it to mirror mainstream methods of teaching and materials

The rationale behind the new literacy programs, was based upon the author's experiences not only as a specialist Teacher of the Deaf, but as a schoolboy between the years 1944 – 1955 and a mainstream teacher from the years 1966 – 1971. Consideration of the pre-A.R.R.O.W. learning experiences, born of well established teaching methodologies, provides valuable insight into the development of the Self-Voice recording approach.

Pre-A.R.R.O.W. School Experiences

During the author's schooling and also during his early years as a teacher, several features of classroom methodologies were commonplace. Classes were large – even as a teacher in 1966 the author's first class consisted of 42, Year 3 Primary School pupils. Pupils sat in rows and were directed to text mostly presented on a blackboard. Blackboard material was often differentiated, according to ability, by the use of coloured chalks for various levels of difficulty. Reading aloud from a blackboard or text books, either as a class, group-by-group, or individually, was standard educational practice, as was chanting of material needing to be rote learnt. Inherent within these activities was of course, the oral tradition, the act of speaking, of talking and directing communication to others, of helping develop internal speech.

Chanting

Material for chanting often included multiplication tables, facts and information, choral passages and poems. It is felt that the benefits of short periods of chanting should not be ignored, due to several factors:

1. Chanting is a recognised way of effectively learning rote material.
2. Chanting facilitates the use of the Self-Voice.
3. A feeling of power and togetherness is engendered within a group when chanting material.
4. Chanting encourages the development of the articulatory loop which links the sound system to the organs used in speech production.
5. The right hemisphere brain functions, dealing with the suprasegmental aspects of speech and language, are also utilised when chanting is conducted in a strong, familiar, rhythmic manner.

National Speech Standards

It is reported by a leading charity for speech and language development, 'I Can', that according to a YouGov poll conducted in late 2009, one child in six between the age of 1 and 6, has difficulty in learning to talk. In a press release News Centre Dcsf 15th Oct 2009, the government appointed Communication Champion for Children, Jean Gross, stressed the importance of speech and language development during school years:

"...Good communication skills are vital. Without them children have little chance of getting good GCSE's or getting a decent job..."

It is felt by the author that there are many factors influencing the high incidence of speech problems in the UK, but again would reiterate that, with Special Needs pupils, virtually all of whom were experiencing communication difficulties, vocalisation skills were shown to improve by some 38.87% within 10 hours A.R.R.O.W. (Ibid). The power of A.R.R.O.W. to enhance the communication skills of adults with severe speech and language problems, will be discussed in Chapter 8, but undoubtedly confirms the potential of A.R.R.O.W. Self-Voice to help attack the problems experienced by many pre and post school age pupils/adults.

Introducing A.R.R.O.W. Reading and Spelling Programs

A.R.R.O.W. Reading/Spelling programs were introduced into mainstream schools in 1986. The programs were markedly influenced by the author's previous experiences as a pupil at school, mainstream teacher and Teacher of the Deaf when using A.R.R.O.W. with Special Needs students. It was decided to base the first A.R.R.O.W. mainstream school literacy programs on the use of High Frequency words which were introduced within short passages based upon the Four Seasons - 'Spring', 'Summer', 'Autumn' and 'Winter'. Comprehension questions were included at the close of each passage and were based upon the textual material. Any mis-copied words were written out three times as an aide memoire at the foot of each Topic.

Spring in the Town
In a town Spring can be very good. The shops may have new things to sell. The shopkeepers have all been busy. A boy called John is in town. John could do with new shoes. He has an old pair. He looks at the shoe shops, he looks at his money. John has about ten pounds.

1. Can spring be good in a town?
2. Do the shops have new things to sell?
3. Who have been busy?
4. Does John need new shoes?
5. Where does John look?
6. What also does John look at?
7. How much money does John have?

The problems of writing a Topic around specific High Frequency Words are evident. Some sentences appear 'baked' and somewhat unnatural when inserted within a limited-sentence Topic framework. Since these early programs, it has been found easier to include High Frequency Words within words, sentences and more expansive Topics now included in the latest DVD programs. In the early Topics, and selected DVD programs, the pupil could, if they wish, record an answer to a recorded question, then write out the appropriate response on Self-Voice replay.

Poetry

A selection of poems were also included within the Reading/Spelling programs. The poems were usually short in length, with the text first being spoken in its entirety, then broken into recordable sections for the student to repeat.

My Dog
My dog's nice,
He's brown and white
And runs everywhere.
He barks at birds,

He talks to me,
He can climb our tree
Honest!

During 2012 the poems' master recordings for the learners to follow were re-recorded by pupils and a teacher from Scoil Bhride Clane Eire. This development proved very successful and pupils from countries other than Southern Ireland have responded most positively to the lilting Irish Tutor Voices.

Spellings
High Frequency words were pre-recorded and presented on a tape as word lists which the student repeated one word at a time then named the letters within each word. On a separate tape the words were placed into sentences which were repeated in their entirety by the student.

A.R.R.O.W. Procedures, Failure of Cascading and Need for Tutor Training
All audio-cassette programs were pre-recorded in the traditional A.R.R.O.W. manner allowing set procedures to be followed. The pattern was therefore multi-sensory, in which a student listened, recorded, replayed the Self-Voice and during replay took dictation whilst looking at the textual material. After successful trialling in Somerset schools, a commercial package of books, pre-recorded tapes and a comprehensive instruction manual was marketed nationally. It quickly became apparent that a 'shelf selling' exercise, linked to cascading the concept to other teachers, was not achieving the desired results in terms of effectiveness of the A.R.R.O.W. system and that Tutor Training was essential in order to maintain standards.

The current A.R.R.O.W. Tutor Manual (p 6) stresses the need for training...
"A.R.R.O.W. does not cascade...A.R.R.O.W. is involved with deep neurological processes and great care must be taken to recognise this. A.R.R.O.W. tutors are obtaining results hardly ever achieved with other approaches using similar numbers of students or within the timescale given to A.R.R.O.W."

Several decades after the decision was reached to supply A.R.R.O.W. materials only in conjunction with a training program, present-day tutors still confirm the need to undergo instruction and practice from a 'Trainer of Tutors', prior to implementing the technique with their students.

The Use of a Tutor and Single A.R.R.O.W. Cassette Recorder
Despite a most encouraging initial introduction with mainstream pupils at the host school, the potential of A.R.R.O.W. to reach a wide spread population was restricted by the use of pre-recorded tapes which required a special two track recorder similar to those used in the author's Hearing Impaired classroom. Most schools could only afford one such recorder, thereby limiting the number of students helped by the approach. In 1990, it was decided to break away from a pattern of "off the shelf" selling. A.R.R.O.W. training began to include less restricted recording options in addition to those arising from the

use of pre-recorded tapes.

In post-1990 recording techniques, the author established that the student's own voice could be recorded on a special "master" two track recorder, but the recording could then be played on less expensive but more widely available, standard cassette players. The tutor and student sat side by side wearing headsets, in order to make a recording. A.R.R.O.W. material was extensively revised and additional material now included differentiated passages of information and precision spellings based upon word families. The word families were grouped according to the number of letters within each word, together with their level of difficulty. The central role of an A.R.R.O.W. tutor therefore moved away from speech/language development and became one of helping the student make as perfect a recording as possible when following the differentiated spellings and prose passages of information. The tutor's role as 'adviser and mentor' continues today and is never more evident than when using the Free Field technique for developing story telling, diary keeping, description skills and revision techniques.

Disadvantages of the A.R.R.O.W. Audio Cassette System
Even with the later audio cassette approach, it became apparent that the system was relatively expensive in terms of tutor time and was clearly not as cost effective as the later computer operating system. The audio cassette approach required 1:1 support from a trained teacher in order for each student to have their voice recorded with appropriately graded material. A high level of operator skill was sometimes required during recording and it was necessary to continually assess each student's requirements during the recording session. Group work meant that each student needed to access a cassette recorder with headphones and manipulate both the recorder, text book on stand and exercise book for eye-level referencing of text. Some students had difficulty in simultaneously tracking text from a book and operating the cassette player/recorder when undertaking dictation. The system was somewhat bulky, required over 20 cassettes to cover the material, and needed expensive add-on support hardware in order to implement the movie or visual speech functions that had been first introduced almost ten years previously in 1975.

The Emergence of Computer Technology
Schools were introducing computer technology during the late 1970's. Computers immediately showed that they had a greater appeal for students than the somewhat limited audio cassette systems, although they did not at the time have a Self-Voice recording facility. The author devised a programming pattern taken from a computer's instruction manual, in which the student referenced the screen text, recorded the question and answer on the A.R.R.O.W. cassette player, then punched in the appropriate Yes/No response on the computer which confirmed the accuracy of the response, in phrase or sentence format.

By 2000 it was obvious that the way forward for A.R.R.O.W. was a total commitment to computerised A.R.R.O.W. learning techniques. The introduction of the digital Self-Voice A.R.R.O.W. programs developed in conjunction with Aaron Gunstone, involved years of ongoing research. The advantages became obvious:

- Echoing and Split Record techniques were more accurately produced using digitalised computer controls and were far easier to learn by Trainee Tutors.
- Students were able work in groups without the need for tutor 1:1 when recording their voices and more readily accepted the use of the latest computer based technologies.
- A.R.R.O.W. material was stored within a computer rather than needing bulky hardcopy books and tapes.
- Movement between levels of material was far quicker.
- Movies were reintroduced into the A.R.R.O.W. system after a 20 year gap and considerably enhanced the free writing and language learning approach to A.R.R.O.W.
- Colour background, text highlighting and text enlargement facilities linked to the voice recordings, greatly aided those students with tracking and/or other processing problems.
- The use of computer technology increased the range and flexibility of tutors' and students' skills and gave a far more professional presentation of material.

Topics
Tutor Voice recordings have been made of passages of information termed 'Topics' which are differentiated from pre-reader levels to those of a reading age above 13+ years. The Tutor voice speaks a phrase or sentence which is afterwards recorded by the student. Any errors in production can be re-recorded as correct speech patterns by the student. In some passages a long sentence can be divided into two or three sections for recording purposes using Split Record techniques. In such cases, the natural pause and flow of the sentence are maintained within each section, yet the sentence is presented as a complete item on Self-Voice replay. Some topics contain comprehension-type questions based on the written text. More advanced programs contain questions which require the use of inference and reasoning in order to answer questions appropriately. In the A.R.R.O.W. work sessions, the student undertakes dictation from the recorded Self-Voice whilst referencing the text then marks each word copied correctly. Any words not copied correctly are written out three times at the foot of the page.

Topics are based upon real life themes with interest and ability levels which are appropriate for students of both genders ranging from non-readers to University level students. Currently, over 50 graded Topics are available for students and these contribute towards a total in excess of 150+ A.R.R.O.W. literacy lessons. This quantity of work covers a far greater number of A.R.R.O.W. sessions than any students have undertaken to date.

Topics - Non Access to Text When Recording
Tutors have the facility to mask or delete text so that a more able student does not have the written form available when recording or taking dictation. After dictation is complete, the student can refer to the original text material for purposes of marking the accuracy of their responses.

Grammatical Error Work
The A.R.R.O.W. tutor has the facility to set up Topics which reinforce the use of grammatical rules. Standard A.R.R.O.W. text can be modified so that the student is required to correct error patterns specifically inserted within a Topic by a tutor. The student records the correct sentence/paragraph but is then presented with an incorrect written pattern. Afterwards the student corrects the faulty sample of text when undertaking dictation and refers to the original, correctly written Topic in order to check the accuracy of any corrections.

A.R.R.O.W. Pre-Reader and Free Field Techniques
The material covers a wide age and ability range for reading, spelling and communication skills. The format also greatly enhances A.R.R.O.W. use for pupils needing to meet or consolidate pre-reading experiences.

The approach for the pre-reader requires 1:1 teaching in which the pupil and tutor sit alongside each other wearing headsets. The pupil looks at movie sequences, or works on a separate stimulus generated spontaneously from the pupil's own interest or ideas. The tutor helps the student formulate and record a relevant phrase or sentence and this is typed out by the tutor/student and recorded in attainable parts by the student through Split Recording processes. The student then listens to the replayed Self-Voice and follows the text as confirmation of learning. The tutor can ask the student to point to appropriate words, phrases or sentences from the text as a further reinforcement. These words are presented by the tutor in a clearly structured fashion which aims to give a student maximum success. A.R.R.O.W. practice sessions, held on another occasion, can further consolidate learning.

Student Centred Language
The importance of student centred language in the acquisition of reading skills is widely acknowledged. The A.R.R.O.W. 'Free Field' approach follows the pattern established for the pre-reader. The tutor and pupil first discuss reading interest material, sometimes perhaps brought in by the student or introduced by the tutor. The tutor elicits verbal responses from the pupil which are then recorded and typed in by the tutor/student as originally given, or are amended into acceptable speech/language structures. The final text then forms the basis for the next phase of learning in which the student is required to read the material 'live' and identify words or phrases from the text which can, if required,

be written into an exercise book or saved as text.

Alphabet
The unique A.R.R.O.W. alphabet learning facility is presented for younger or non-English speaking learners and for those with specific articulation problems. Each letter of the alphabet and word containing that letter, are shown in large size font. The complete alphabet is shown at the foot of the screen with the particular letter highlighted. Each letter is presented either as a sound or as a letter name. A movie sequence relates to the sound or letter and word being introduced. 'B' for 'Bus', shows a movie of a bus, 'D' for 'Dog', shows a movie of a dog etc. A pre-recorded Tutor voice gives the sound/letter name and the word to be repeated. The student copies the sound/letter name and word, then listens back to the Self-Voice, or indeed both voices, in sequence.

An alphabet song has been pre-recorded as an optional aid for pupils. The song is also shown as a movie sequence featuring a teenager. The song is first presented in its entirety, followed by each line of the song being presented on its own, thereby allowing the pupil to repeat the line and hear themselves singing the Alphabet song on Self-Voice playback.

ABCDEFG, HIJKLMNOP, QRSTUV, WXY and Z
Now you know your ABC,
You can sing along with me.

Spellings
Graded spelling programs contain words of varying length from Consonant Vowel Consonant (CVC) material, through to words of six or seven letters which are themselves, taken from passages of information graded at a 15 year old reading level. Many of the spellings used within the scheme are placed in word families and are included within sentences to aid semantic processes. In essence, the process is similar to that adopted for Topic recording. The computer Tutor voice speaks the necessary words and sounds or letters to be named, before they are recorded by the student.

Five short vowels, a, e, i, o, u are presented in Consonant Vowel Consonant format (CVC), e.g. 'bat', 'cat', 'fat'... These are delivered in a synthetic or analytic manner within a CVC pattern.
Synthetic approach - sounds first then word name - c.a.t., cat, b.a.t., bat,
Analytic approach - word first then individual sounds - cat, c.a.t., bat, b.a.t.
As a further aid to learning, the vowel is colour coded within each stand-alone CVC word.
Each word is then put into context within sentences. 'My cat is here', 'Put the bat down'.

Non-sense vowel consonant vowel 'pseudo' words
Work has been conducted with 'non-sense' words using sounds and written symbols. Students see and hear cvc words of no meaning e.g. 'cas', 'han', 'zel',

'pex', 'wid', 'sig', 'lod', 'wof', 'tul', 'ruv' and record these as part of their phonic build/relationships.

High and Medium Frequency Words
It is widely acknowledged that direct visual access is important to reading and therefore all pupils should be able to maximise their sight vocabulary, particularly of frequently used words such as 'big', 'come', 'get', 'in', 'went'. The word is first recorded on its own, the word's letters are named, then the word is placed within a sentence, 'Look at that big car', 'Can you come?' Medium Frequency words such as 'about', 'began', 'being', 'above', 'across', are treated in the same manner of presentation. First the word is spoken, it's letters named, then it is included within a sentence, e.g. 'about', 'It is about here', 'began', 'She began to walk away'.

Personal Spelling Profile System
The Personal Spelling Profile (PSP) system is central to the A.R.R.O.W. Self-Voice spelling approach. The Personal Spelling Profile system mirrors a teaching strategy from the 1950's–1960's when a student took written work in an exercise book to the teacher during a lesson. The teacher would mark the work, with the child present, and identify spelling error patterns for the student to correct. This old, but effective teaching strategy has been adapted by A.R.R.O.W. to computer usage. Over 120 examples of English word families are included within the Personal Spelling Profile system. In the current PSP methodology, a student is assessed using a specially designed test. In essence, the test establishes which word families cause problems for the student. The test is marked and error patterns are afterwards plotted on a matrix by a tutor. The student consults the matrix and identifies which programs to follow. Word families are colour coded within a screen of text and presented as sound recordings with strong rhythmic patterns. The spelling presentation follows the well established A.R.R.O.W. format. It has been found that approximately 75% of spellings acquired through the Personal Spelling Profile system are retained by pupils, without using extensive revision strategies. Students like the straightforward nature of the system, the immediate feedback of progress and the fact that they are not over-learning material which they already know. As noted previously the PSP word families are colour coded and all relevant spellings are placed within sentences as a further aid to learning. The PSP principle is also applied to more Advanced Spellings in which word families proving difficult for a student are placed within appropriate sections which may/may not include the rules governing their constructions. Research conducted in 2018 reveals a prescribed number of PSP sections (9-12) will greatly improve reading/spelling performances.

High Ability Level Spellings
Some students are above the ability level of word family acquisition and undertake the learning of more difficult spellings. These are taken from Advanced Level Topics and include words for those with a spelling age exceeding 10+ years. A part sample of an Advanced Level Topic is given:

Honey Bees
Only Honey Bees make honey which everyday people can use. In order to obtain honey, the Worker, or female bee, puts a long tube-like tongue deep inside a flower. She sucks out the nectar and stores the nectar in her honey stomach. After an industrious time working and flying, she gives the nectar to a House Bee ... continued

A Topic based upon 'Honey Bees', is therefore, followed by the learning of spellings taken from the particular Topic e.g. 'honey', 'nectar', 'tongue', 'millions', 'tube-like', 'stomach' 'amazing'... The A.R.R.O.W. 'word first–then letters named' spelling format continues throughout this level.

Curriculum Based Spellings – Free Field Facility
'Curriculum Specific' words, met during a student's area of study, may be prepared by the tutor as part of A.R.R.O.W. The words can be produced and saved as a document by the tutor, recalled when required, and pasted into the Free Field section of the A.R.R.O.W. work options. The student can then undertake learning of the material using the Self-Voice facility. A set of Science key words for example, could readily include 'Celsius', 'Fahrenheit', 'temperature', 'heat loss', 'thermometer', 'beaker', 'spatula', 'boiling', 'condensation'. The spellings can, if required, be placed in carrier sentences by the tutor or able student.

Spelling Rules
The A.R.R.O.W. spelling scheme includes rules which cover the following,
Singulars, Plurals, Phonemes, Syllables, Consonants, Prefixes, Suffixes, Homophones, Letter Strings, Unstressed Vowels, Silent Consonants, Root Words and Apostrophes. These examples are treated in the usual A.R.R.O.W. manner of word presentation, letter names and inclusion within sentences. The pupil looks at the text, hears and records after the Tutor voice, then takes dictation from the Self-Voice. Work is afterwards checked for accuracy of copying.

System Flexibility – Timescales used for the Application of A.R.R.O.W.
Literacy skill improvements for students of all ages and abilities have been achieved and sustained under many timetable applications. The flexibility of A.R.R.O.W. is such that it operates very successfully under any of the following 3-8 hour formats, with the proviso that the pupils undertake the necessary amount of work.

1. Daily A.R.R.O.W. program. On a daily session of 30-45 minutes for 5-10 days.
2. A.R.R.O.W. delivered two or three times a week for several weeks with 30-45 minute sessions.
3. One set of A.R.R.O.W. programs per week for five weeks involving 1 hour per session for elder or more able pupils only.

4. Distance Learning. After an initial assessment by a qualified A.R.R.O.W. tutor, students undertake the programs at home.
5. Intensive single session training for mature students, totalling 2+ hours.

The Format of the Tutor Training Program
The Tutor Training Program course is split into three main sections.
The first section of the course covers two days and is essentially one in which the trainee tutor becomes competent in the use of the appropriate assessment procedures, DVD material and equipment. The second section of the course requires the trainee tutor to work with students. It is expected that trainee tutors will work with a minimum of 5 students and trainees will be required to provide evidence through test results of their effectiveness when undertaking A.R.R.O.W. with their students. The final section of the course requires a trainee tutor to continue to work with a minimum of 5 students then submit a report based upon their A.R.R.O.W. project. On receipt of this report, tutors are accredited as A.R.R.O.W. tutors. In order to remain a certificated A.R.R.O.W. tutor it is necessary for tutors to submit annual data of results from at least 5 students per annum.

Trainer of Tutors Course
In order to become a Trainer of Tutors, the tutor must have acquired the necessary A.R.R.O.W. skills when working with students and have completed the A.R.R.O.W. Tutor Course before undertaking a period of further training and observation from established Tutor Trainers.

Andrew Washbrooke, a Tutor trainer reports:
"... I have trained tutors ranging from Teaching Assistants to Specialist Advisory Teachers within Inclusion Support Services. During training, usually by lunchtime on Day 1, the student tutors start to realise how A.R.R.O.W. can be used and begin to mention students they intend to start working with. The majority of tutors start to become very excited about the prospect of using A.R.R.O.W. Due to the careful structure of training, the tutors gain full understanding of the system and the various techniques which can be applied to a vast range of students. Training normally takes place over 2 consecutive days and by the end of Day 2 the majority of tutors agree they would not have had the confidence or ability to use A.R.R.O.W. without the formal training. It is generally true that if any of the student tutors are sceptical about A.R.R.O.W. prior to training, once they complete their first cohort of students, they become some of the strongest supporters."

Chapter 5 Conclusion
A.R.R.O.W. methodologies proved that various literacy skills could be improved including consonant discrimination, sentence understanding, Short Term Memory and speech/communication. A Self-Voice literacy program was designed based upon the author's experiences as a child at school and as a Mainstream/Specialist teacher. The importance of chanting as a teaching/ learning tool is noted together with the decline of speech skills amongst pre and

early school years children. A.R.R.O.W. programs were introduced based upon Topics of information and High Frequency Key Words, Spellings and Poems. Cascading had previously proven an ineffective way of disseminating A.R.R.O.W. Self-Voice and thus Tutor Training became essential. The specialised two track recording equipment was adapted to use standard cassette players but still required considerable operator skill and individual tuition. The emergence of computer technology enhanced A.R.R.O.W. in terms of recording/playback techniques. Group work was central to A.R.R.O.W. with a great lessening of the need for 1:1 work. The introduction of movies, coloured background and text highlighting took the approach to new levels, as did graded computer based Topics centred upon 'real life' themes. Error identification/correction tasks were introduced. Free field programs cover spontaneous student centred language outputs which are played back to form part of language and written processes. The Alphabet learning component, features large size letters, movies for each alphabet sound and a song covering the letters of the alphabet. Spelling programs range from CVC combinations treated in Analytic or Synthetic formats, Non-Sense CVC words, High and Medium Frequency words and the unique Personal Spelling Profile system (PSP). The PSP parallels previous tried and trusted teaching methods in which a class teacher marked pupils' work during a lesson, then set up an individualised family of spellings to be learnt, based upon the student's errors. These principles are also applied within more difficult material. More able students are allocated spellings to be learned from individual words taken from Advanced Topics. Curriculum based tutor prepared spellings can be pasted into the free-field area of the program. The Major Rules of Spellings and their applications across a wide range of abilities are treated within the global spelling scheme. The great flexibility of A.R.R.O.W. Self-Voice and the timescales for delivery, mean that the approach can be applied either in a single 2 hour slot for the more able, used during single 30-40 minute sessions for several consecutive days, split into several lessons applied across a varying number of weeks, or applied in the Distance Learning format described previously. The two-day Tutor Training Program is sectionalised and requires each tutor to use A.R.R.O.W. with a minimum of 5 students before submitting a report centred upon the work undertaken, results gained and reactions of the students.

Chapter 6
Evidence of Literacy Improvements

Accepted Effectiveness of A.R.R.O.W. Programs - Departmental Approval . 69

Independent A.R.R.O.W. Research 69
    Results 69

Eire Study A.R.R.O.W. 70

A Non-A.R.R.O.W. Self-Voice Study - Word Recognition Improvements 70
    Results 71

A.R.R.O.W. Self Voice Evidence: 71

A.R.R.O.W. Reading and Spelling Improvements: Primary Schools 72
    Results 72

Groundbreaking Evidence From Years 1 and 2 72

South West Primary School. Results after 2-3 hours A.R.R.O.W. 73

Pre-intervention Performance for Reading and Spelling 73

Organisation of the One Week Intervention 73

Differentiation and Pupil Needs 74

Spelling Control Group 74

Additional Tests 74

Neale Analysis Reading Ability - Word Attack Skills 75

Comprehension Skills 75

Reading Rate 75

Weschler WORD Spelling Test 75

Pupil Attitude and Self-Esteem 75

English as an Additional Language at Home 76

Leicester Pilot Project 76

Literacy Improvements with Average/Above Average Primary School Pupils 77

Results after 2-3 Hours A.R.R.O.W. Wigan Primary School 77

Results after 7+ Hours A.R.R.O.W. Rhondda Valley Primary School 78

The Taunton Project 2017 See appendices 38 - 39 78

Reading and Spelling Improvements: Secondary Schools/Colleges 78

A.R.R.O.W. Intervention at a South West Community College 80

Pre-intervention Performance for Reading and Spelling 80

Organisation of the One Week Intervention 80

Differentiation and Pupil Needs 80

Results after 3-4 Hours A.R.R.O.W. 80

Chapter 6 Conclusion 81

Chapter 6
Evidence of Literacy Improvements

This chapter investigates the effectiveness of A.R.R.O.W. within the educational sector. Evidence will be presented from school/college age students in Eire, England, Wales and Trinidad. Most of the evidence is supplied from tutors relatively new to A.R.R.O.W. working with students who have not met the approach before.

Accepted Effectiveness of A.R.R.O.W. Programs - Departmental Approval
The Department for children schools and families, have issued a publication "What works for pupils with literacy difficulties" (Brookes and NFER 2007). In the publication, A.R.R.O.W. is evaluated as a scheme for reading and spelling at Primary level. A ratio of 1 would be normal progress, i.e. 1 month gain in reading/spelling after 1 month's work. A.R.R.O.W. however, far surpassed this ratio for both reading and spelling. The Dcsf evaluation (p133) shows ratio gains of 16.5 for reading accuracy and 14.1 for spelling accuracy.

"The ratio gains show that this amount of progress in 1½ weeks was remarkable, if not spectacular." Since the 2007 publication, evidence is to hand which shows that A.R.R.O.W. sites have even exceeded this rate of progress (Brooks 5th ed. 2016 pp 21) (Lane 2018 Appendix 38 pp 160).

Independent A.R.R.O.W. Research
See appendix 12
An A.R.R.O.W. literacy project was conducted by Andrew Richards at the School of Education Exeter University in 2008. The research involved all Year 6 pupils (n=85) at a Bristol Primary School. A standard A.R.R.O.W.™ 10 hour group-based program was followed across a 2 week period in which pupils attended daily for a 1 hour per day. Assessment of progress was gauged by a pre and post intervention application of the WORD assessment measure (Weschler, D 1993).

Results
The research showed that over a fortnightly intervention period, the Year 6 students made marked progress in reading (1.36 yrs.), spelling (0.7 yrs.) and comprehension skills (1.88 yrs.). It was found that the 1 hour session was the maximum time students could maintain attention. All recommendations to tutors since this work, have stressed the need for pupils to take a break from the A.R.R.O.W. task if following such a concentrated training schedule. Despite

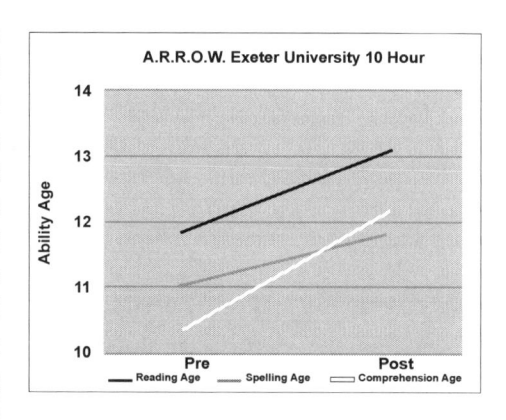

the demands of a daily 1 hour lesson, students were enthusiastic about their progress, one student commenting:

"It's good, it like injects it into your brain straight away and it's fun."

Another student stated:
"You learn more better when listening to your own voice."

Throughout this period continuing support was given by Professor Bob Burden, University of Exeter, who had long appreciated the worth of Self-Voice work.

Eire Study A.R.R.O.W.

Dr. Mary Nugent Senior Educational Psychologist Eire, headed a project evaluating several literacy interventions. including A.R.R.O.W. within two Secondary and two Primary schools. Total population receiving help was some eighty-five students with an average age 11 years 4 months. One Girls' Secondary school had a range of students including Travellers, non-nationals and students from disadvantaged communities. The other was a mixed community school based in a rural area. One of the Primary Schools had a varied intake whilst the second was a rural mixed primary school. A.R.R.O.W was delivered by eleven trained teachers to a student population which included those with Dyslexia and Mild General Learning Difficulties.

It was reported that the A.R.R.O.W. students spent on average seven hours and nine minutes on the Self-Voice work. Mary Nugent reports that, dependent upon which assessment tests were used, the A.R.R.O.W. students achieved between 9 and 11 months progress with reading and 4 to 6 months progress in spelling after just 7 hours.

She additionally makes the strong point that when teacher time is taken into consideration, evaluations against 1 hour of tuition show A.R.R.O.W. to be 57% more effective for reading and 24% more effective for spelling than the next closest intervention.

Questionnaires were sent to teachers on the benefits of A.R.R.O.W.

Dr Nugent writes
'In terms of the benefits of A.R.R.O.W teachers overwhelmingly commented on the progress that students made in reading and spelling...The other main area of positive comment was about the students enjoyment or pride in the work...This programme can therefore be offered to relatively large numbers of children and may be a useful way of raising reading standards in our schools.'

A Non-A.R.R.O.W. Self-Voice Study - Word Recognition Improvements

An independent study undertaken by Exeter University was based upon non-A.R.R.O.W. Self-Voice work (Mcleod, F.J. et al, 2008). The researchers investigated whether an audio Self-Voice system, first developed by a British manufacturer, Coomber Electronics, in conjunction with A.R.R.O.W., would facilitate phonic awareness in terms of word recognition. The project, conducted entirely independently of A.R.R.O.W., would of course confirm/reject the efficacy of using the Self-Voice as a learning strategy.

The research project was based in Devon Primary Schools with an opportunity sample of 159 students aged 6-13 years of mixed gender and ability. Teaching Assistants received a 15 hour, three day training program before delivering an intervention and also undertook pre and post assessments of the pupils.

Pupils received 20 sessions of 20 minutes input, totalling 8-9 hours spread across 10 weeks plus pre and post assessment time. In essence pupils were helped to record lists of words then listened back to these whilst referencing the lists and repeated the lists aloud minus the recording. The word lists used analytic and synthetic presentation. Another control group listened to an adult (Female) voice on tape saying the same lists of words. Assessment of progress was established by using The Boder Test of Reading/Spelling Patterns and Neale Analysis of Reading.

Results
37 pupils in the Self-Voice group averaged greater gains than 36 pupils using another voice and 35 pupils in normal classroom routine group. Self-Voice groups achieved 1.1 months S.D. 0.42. The superiority of the Self-Voice group was statistically significant. Investigation of the data showed that girls gained slightly more than boys and older pupils benefited more than younger pupils.

The study showed the superiority of the Self-Voice if compared to other voices in literacy learning tasks. In this respect the project closely emulated A.R.R.O.W. Self- Voice work conducted some 10 years earlier. It has been noted in Chapter 4 that Lane and Chinn (ibid) established the primacy of the Self–Voice, rather than another voice, for rote learning of multiplication tables. Vile (ibid) also found that word list recall with University students was more effective when using Self-Voice rather than another voice.

A.R.R.O.W. Self Voice Evidence:
Data submitted to A.R.R.O.W. from tutors, reveals the extent of progress made across the age range and with groups of varying ability students. In total, evidence is taken from 1,207 students based at 54 schools/colleges in Eire, England, Wales, Trinidad and Tobago. This progress will be considered within two main groups, notably students at Primary Schools and those attending Secondary School/College provision.

A.R.R.O.W. Reading and Spelling Improvements: Primary Schools

Results
See appendix 13
Evidence is taken from 779 students in 35 Primary Schools in Eire, England, Wales and Trinidad. These students undertook the standard 10 hour A.R.R.O.W. DVD group based programs.

- Age range 7+ to 11+ years. Average age: 10 years
- Average reading deficit was 15 months below chronological age
- Average spelling deficit was 18 months below chronological age
- Average improvement for reading (word attack) was 9 months
- Average improvement for spelling was 5 months

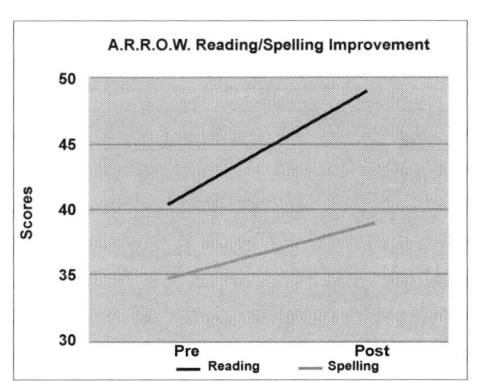

Evidence shows there is a pronounced average improvement of 9 months reading - word recognition and 5 months spelling skills after maximum A.R.R.O.W. intervention of 10 hours.

It should be noted that evidence presented later in this chapter confirms the long held view that A.R.R.O.W. reading and spelling skills in effect, begin to improve within 2-3 hours of commencing the programs and that improvements are sustained across 2-3 months. Reading and spelling skills further improve after a second intervention of similar or even less time.

Analysis of results from the UK, Ireland and the West Indies, shows that above average children can make the greatest monthly improvements within just a few hours of commencing A.R.R.O.W. Virtually all children of average and below average literacy performance, also make marked progress for reading and spelling. If their improvements are related to previous performances throughout their school careers, then the A.R.R.O.W. effect is pronounced. After a number of years in the educational system, in which a worrying gap develops between chronological age and actual performance, most pupils using A.R.R.O.W. are finally showing an upward and encouraging rate of progress. The benefits to the student and savings to a school are obvious. The evidence suggests that some children may only require one A.R.R.O.W. intervention, others however, may need 2-3 or even more block sessions, before their A.R.R.O.W. performances are optimised.

Groundbreaking Evidence From Years 1 and 2
Information released from Bolton and Wigan Primary Schools shows that A.R.R.O.W. literacy improvements can be effected with pupils in years 1 and 2, who are as young as 6-7 years of age. The pupils at three schools (n=27)

worked in groups of 5 or 1:1 with a tutor, in two or three 30-60 minute sessions for 3-4 weeks. Standard A.R.R.O.W. material was used with pupils ranging across a 4 year ability level of reading and/or spelling. Average pre-A.R.R.O.W. reading scores were 21.92 whilst average pre-A.R.R.O.W. spelling scores were 19.81. Average reading scores post-A.R.R.O.W. moved to 31.86 a relative increase of 10 months progress. Average spelling scores post-A.R.R.O.W. were 25.48 thereby showing a relative increase of 6 months progress. The tutor's report that the standard A.R.R.O.W. computer-based material was followed and the 6+ year old pupils, once they became familiar with the requirements, worked the approach on their own. The implications are considerable for any young pupils who are at risk of developing poor literacy skills. Early A.R.R.O.W. intervention, as experienced by the Wigan and Bolton pupils, can well prevent the cycle of failure which blights too many pupils' reading and writing skills and invariably leads to low academic achievement. Use of A.R.R.O.W. with young pupils can also evidently maximise the word attack and spelling skills for pupils of average or above average ability as well as those with evident literacy problems.

South West Primary School. Results after 2-3 hours A.R.R.O.W.
See appendix 14

An opportunity sample of 23 pupils from Year 5, comprising 13 male and 10 female pupils participated in a 1 week A.R.R.O.W. project. The sample included students of average and above average literacy skills as well as those with literacy problems. A group of students for whom English is an Additional Language were included within the selected sample. Pre-intervention reading and spelling tests were administered prior to the commencement of the one week project.

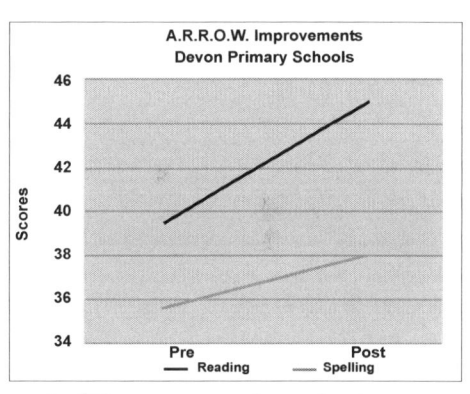

Pre-intervention Performance for Reading and Spelling
The reading score for word attack skills realised an average of 39.43. This represents a reading age of 8 years 8 months i.e. well over 12 months below the average chronological age of the students. Initial spelling scores averaged 35.52, a spelling age of 8 years 6 months, i.e. some 18 months behind the students' average chronological age.

Organisation of the One Week Intervention
Pupils attended a maximum of 40 minutes per session in groups of five and worked with minimal supervision. The first session included an introduction to A.R.R.O.W. The final session included post intervention reading and self-esteem tests. The over viewing tutor usually focused on each pupil's reading, spelling and self-checking for 2-3 minutes per session, otherwise the pupils worked independently.

Differentiation and Pupil Needs

Students' individual A.R.R.O.W. work programs were graded according to their reading and spelling ability which varied widely. The least able student had a reading age of 5 years 9 months, whilst the most able had a reading age of 11 years, i.e. between 5-6 years in advance of the least able reader. The lowest ability speller scored at a level of 6 years 7 months, compared to the most able who scored at a level of 11 years 4 months. It was not uncommon for pupils working on A.R.R.O.W. within a group, to have a 5 year range of ability. Included amongst the sample were six students for whom English is an Additional Language at home, students with Dyslexia or other literacy problems and a student with marked Behavioural Problems within the mainstream classroom. It was most encouraging that all students made progress in reading and/or spelling. At the lowest end of the ability spectrum, an English as an Additional Language student realised a 100% improvement in word attack skills whilst the least able of the English mother tongue achievers, improved 17% on his previous score.

After A.R.R.O.W. intervention, the reading scores had progressed from a pre-intervention average of 39.43, 8 years 8 months, to 45.04, a reading age of 9 years 2 months, i.e. the pupils averaged 6 months improvement inside the 2-3 hour, 1 week program. This result compares very favourably with those A.R.R.O.W. results gained throughout the UK with mixed ability children of 9-10+ years.

Marked spelling improvements were also evident. After A.R.R.O.W. Self-Voice intervention, spelling scores rose from 35.52 to 38.17, showing a 4 month improvement in spelling across the 2-3 hour programs. Again, the score improvements creditably reflect those obtained elsewhere, given the brevity of the intervention programs.

Spelling Control Group

Eight students from the feeder class could not participate as part of the experimental group and were used as a control group for the pilot. They were tested at the same time and in the same classroom as the experimental group. Their average scores after their first spelling test realised 44.75. Their second spelling test scores gave a mean of 44.5 i.e. a slight reduction from their initial spelling scores and they therefore showed no comparable 4 months spelling improvement as realised by the A.R.R.O.W. group.

Additional Tests

The school decided to implement two additional tests. The Neale Analysis of Reading Ability (Neale, M.D. 1999) and Weschler WORD Spelling Test (Ibid), were independently administered by qualified school staff. A selected sample of 7 students was taken from the experimental group of 23 A.R.R.O.W. students. The 7 students were of mixed ability and results showed the similarity between inter-test results in terms of the performance of specific students.

Neale Analysis Reading Ability - Word Attack Skills
See appendix 15
It was shown that using the Neale Analysis test, marked word attack improvements of 10.5 months were gained within the 2-3 hour programs.

Comprehension Skills
The effects of the 2-3 hour programs were significant for comprehension. Gains of 16 months were realised and set a new benchmark in terms of student expectation. The results mirror those gained in an earlier experiment by Exeter University using Bristol based Year 6 students.

Reading Rate
The independently administered tests also showed that A.R.R.O.W. intervention realised a sharp improvement in the reading rate of those involved in the project. Improvements averaged 18.8 months within the 2-3 hour programs. The recording process, listening to a voice and repeating it whilst accessing text, is inherent to A.R.R.O.W. and undoubtedly had a part to play in the reading rate improvement. It is interesting to note that the act of recording, in which reading aloud is a central component, was placed between good and very good according to the students' A.R.R.O.W. self assessment measures.

Weschler WORD Spelling Test
See appendix 16
The Weschler WORD Spelling Test results, gave gains even higher than those shown using Schonell Spellings. The congruence between the two spelling tests fully supports the data showing that A.R.R.O.W. has effected marked spelling improvements.

Pupil Attitude and Self-Esteem
At the close of a Taunton 2018 project with vulnerable learners, all the pupils undertaking the A.R.R.O.W. intervention were given a self-assessment measure. The students were making their own value judgements of progress prior to knowing the real effects in terms of results. The measure operated within a five point scale from 5 - very good to 1 - very bad. The pupils made a most positive statement about the effects and enjoyment of A.R.R.O.W. The grades shown are averages for all students involved in the 1 week project.

Did you enjoy A.R.R.O.W.?	4.6
Has it helped your reading?	4.5
Has it helped your spelling?	4.4
Did you like recording?	4.5
Did you like writing?	3.9
Did you like marking your work?	4.4

The grades are amongst the highest recorded and confirm that all pupils who completed the course felt it had proved of considerable benefit to them. Evidence from the project confirms the student's judgement.

English as an Additional Language at Home
See appendix 17

Six students for whom English is an Additional Language when at home (EAL), were selected as part of the experimental cohort. The students had varying levels of ability and language skills but met the identical word attack/spelling tests. It can be seen that the EAL students performed at an equivalent standard to other members of the experimental cohort – reading improved by 8 months, spelling by 4 months. In terms of self-esteem/assessment of progress, the EAL students also revealed a marked similarity to other members of the group and to a Taunton based EAL group (Please see Appendix 39).

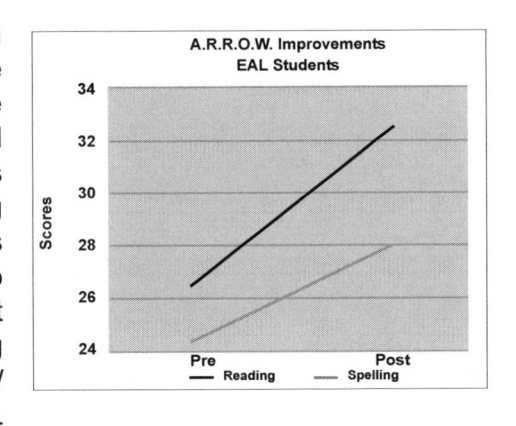

Did you enjoy A.R.R.O.W.?	4.6
Has it helped your reading?	4.5
Has it helped your spelling?	4.0
Did you like recording?	4.6
Did you like writing?	4.3
Did you like marking your work?	4.5

The additional reading and spelling tests, i.e. The Neale Analysis and WORD programs had been employed in the past with A.R.R.O.W. across 10 hour programs but never within a 2-3 hour remit. In this respect, the project was breaking new ground and results revealed a most interesting insight into the immediacy of A.R.R.O.W. for successfully improving comprehension and reading rate skills.

Leicester Pilot Project
A Leicester Primary School undertook a one week investigation into Arrow. A Year 6 class (n=26) was split into two groups viz. an A.R.R.O.W. group (n=13) and a control group (n=13). The two groups were given identical reading and spelling tests pre and post intervention. Results -

After 3 hours work, delivered in one week, it was found that the A.R.R.O.W. group had made 50% greater improvements for reading (+ 6 months realised gain) and 96% greater improvement for *personal performance improvement than the control group. It was also found that the A.R.R.O.W. group made 75% greater improvement for monthly spelling (+ 8 months realised gain) than the controls and 82% greater *personal improvement within the 3 hour DVD program.

* Personal improvement calculated by the difference between final score and original score expressed as a % of original score.

Pupils Rating of A.R.R.O.W.
Pupils self-evaluation of the worth of Arrow was "good" for reading, spelling and recording and virtually replicated the results from the Devon Primary School.

Literacy Improvements with Average/Above Average Primary School Pupils

Following the success of work conducted with mainstream children, particularly those with literacy problems, investigations began into the use of A.R.R.O.W. with average/above average pupils in Primary Schools. The ramifications of the results gained could be of major importance towards raising overall literacy standards throughout schools and colleges.

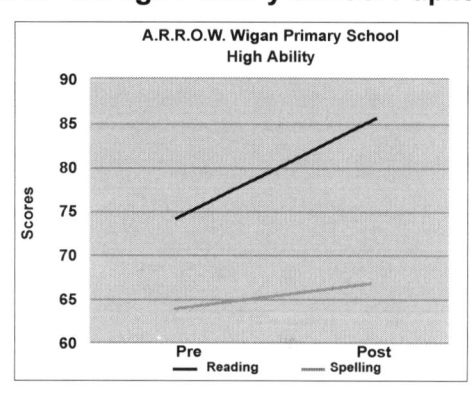

A.R.R.O.W. Wigan Primary School High Ability (chart showing Scores from 60-90, Pre vs Post for Reading and Spelling)

Results after 2-3 Hours A.R.R.O.W. Wigan Primary School
See appendix 18

30 Year 6 students average age 10.8 years, were used in the project. The students averaged 11 years 8 months for reading and were therefore well in advance of their chronological age in terms of word attack skills. Pre-A.R.R.O.W. spelling scores averaged 11 yrs 4 months, showing that the students were again well in advance of their chronological age levels.

In terms of reading and spelling performances, it can be seen that the Year 6 students, already surpassing their actual age for reading and spelling skills, made marked progress within a few hours of commencing the programs. Reading scores reached a test ceiling of +12 yrs 6 months (the upper limit of measurement) realising at least 8 months progress, whilst spelling improved some 4+ months within the 2-3 hour program. On re-testing students a few months later, the school found that A.R.R.O.W. progress was maintained and children continued to improve on a month by month basis.

> *The Headteacher of the school commented at the time:*
> *"We have been absolutely amazed at the rapid sustained progress that our pupils have made. It has made us completely re-think our intervention strategies. Usually if a Yr 5 child aged say 10 years 2 months has a reading age of 12 years 5 months we would normally not provide any intervention yet we are astounded that these high ability children from within a year group have made on average 13 months progress after just 3-4 hours. This shows that A.R.R.O.W. works throughout the school with all abilities of students. The system is now central to our whole-school learning policy."*

Results after 7+ Hours A.R.R.O.W. Rhondda Valley Primary School
See appendix 19

Further improvements of average students, after a short intervention using A.R.R.O.W. were realised again in a South Wales Primary School. The Year 6 pupils were equivalent to their chronological age in terms of word attack skills, yet made marked progress, way in advance of the normal monthly rate. Results showed a 29 months gain in reading and 14 months gain in spelling after 8-10 hours. The A.R.R.O.W. tutor supervising the pupils, was in fact, a Teaching Assistant with a clear perception of the system requirements.

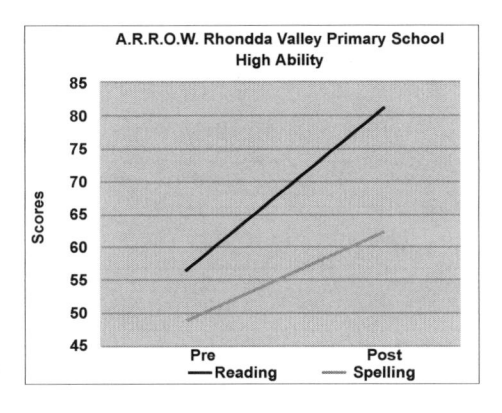

> *The Headteacher of the Rhondda Valley School, confirmed the great progress made by all Year 6 students, in particular the lowest achieving child from the year and highlights the key attributes leading to the great rise in performance:*
>
> *"excellent results...one child improved 8 months in 10 hours and quite frankly, if I'd have had that improvement in a year, I'd have been delighted...it's a combination of the Self-Voice, the programs, old fashioned teaching, the quality of the tutor, the full support of the school."*

The Taunton Project 2017 See appendices 38 - 39

18 students from years 4, 5, 6, attending a Somerset Primary School received 4 hours A.R.R.O.W. delivered in 30 minute sessions across 8 days. Results averaged 9 months reading and 9 months spelling progress. Analysis of results showed that students with English as an Additional Language and those deemed Dyslexic made marked progress. Of particular interest was the finding that the results were gained by students averaging 9 Personal Spelling Profile sections and less than 3 Topics i.e. a pattern for progress emerged from the study.

Reading and Spelling Improvements: Secondary Schools/Colleges

Evidence, at the time of going to press, has been taken from 428 students in 19 Secondary Schools/Colleges. The students undertook the standard 10 hour A.R.R.O.W. DVD programs. Evidence parallels that of Primary aged students and shows a pronounced and rapid improvement in reading and spelling skills after A.R.R.O.W.

Results
See appendix 20

- Age range 11-18+ yrs average age: not available.
- Average reading age was 9 years 5 months, a marked deficit
- Average spelling age was 9 years 3 months, far below an acceptable standard of achievement for Secondary age students
- Average A.R.R.O.W. improvement for reading (word attack) was 8 months after a maximum 10 hour intervention
- Average A.R.R.O.W. improvement for spelling was 5 months after a maximum 10 hour intervention

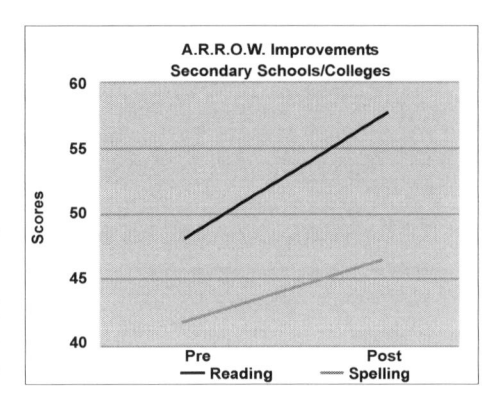

Latest available data confirms the long held view that reading and spelling improve within 2-3 hours of commencing the programs and that literacy skills further improve after a second A.R.R.O.W. intervention of similar length. The evidence suggests that some pupils of secondary age may only require a single intervention, whilst others may need 2-3 or even more, block sessions.

Students of average and below average literacy performance make marked progress for reading and spelling. Taunton based Secondary aged students evaluated A.R.R.O.W. on the five point scale used in other schools i.e. a mark of 5 being 'very good', 1 being 'very bad'. Scores given are averages for the group.

Did you enjoy A.R.R.O.W.?	4.8
Has it helped your reading?	4.3
Has it helped your spelling?	4.4
Did you like recording?	4.5
Did you like writing?	3.8
Did you like marking your work?	4.0

The cohort of Taunton based 12-14 year olds, again confirmed the view that A.R.R.O.W. had improved their reading/spelling skills despite not knowing the actual extent of their progress. The group of students were re-assessed after receiving most positive feedback about their improvements from their tutors. It was found however, that no marked self-appraisal gains were realised following the tutor's comments. It therefore appears that the first judgement of A.R.R.O.W. by these pupils, was a reflective self-appraisal, seemingly independent of feedback from others.

A.R.R.O.W. Intervention at a South West Community College
An A.R.R.O.W. pilot project in a Devon College was initiated in 2008. An

opportunity sample of 24 pupils, 19 male and 5 female pupils, from years 7, 8 and 9 undertook A.R.R.O.W. for 3-4 hours. Pre-intervention reading and spelling tests were administered.

Pre-intervention Performance for Reading and Spelling

The reading score for word attack skills for the 24 pupils realised an average of 44.73. This represents a reading age of 9 years 2 months, i.e. 2-3 years behind the average chronological age for the students. Initial spelling scores averaged 34.87 a spelling age of 8 years 6 months,. i.e. some 3-4 years behind the students' average chronological age.

Organisation of the One Week Intervention

Pupils attended one hour sessions in groups of five and worked with minimal supervision. The over viewing tutor(s) usually focused on each pupil within a group for 2-3 minutes per session otherwise their students worked independently.

Differentiation and Pupil Needs

Students' individual A.R.R.O.W. work programs were graded according to their reading and spelling ability. It was not uncommon for pupils working together in a group, to have a 7 to 8 year ability range. Included amongst the sample were students about to take SATS examinations, students for whom English is an Additional Language at home, students with Dyslexia or other literacy problems, students with Attention problems within the mainstream classroom and a student with Speech/Language difficulties.

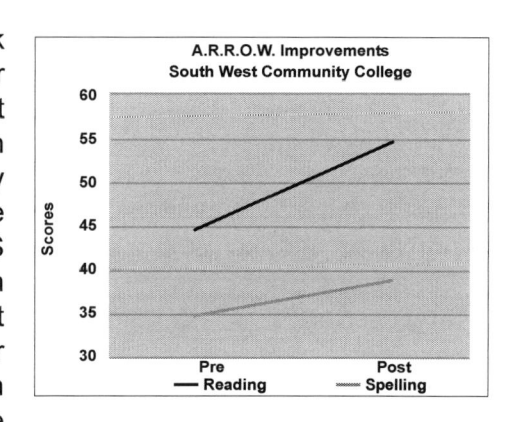

Results after 3-4 Hours A.R.R.O.W.

See appendix 21

It was most encouraging that all students made progress in reading and/or spelling. After A.R.R.O.W. intervention, the average reading scores had progressed to 54.78, a reading age of 9 years 11 months, i.e. the pupils averaged 9 months improvement inside the 3 to 4 hour one week program. Spelling scores rose to 38.41 showing an average 4 month improvement in spelling across the programs. It should be noted that these one week results are amongst the highest recorded within the UK Secondary School system and reflect highly upon the commitment to the project of the students and College staff.

The self-assessment grades were comparable to those recorded elsewhere in the UK and showed that all pupils who completed the course had a most positive attitude to the system. The literacy tutor commendably showed a clear understanding of the nature of the A.R.R.O.W. system and aimed to extend the range of students being helped. She therefore, has initiated a project which also includes non-College, Primary School youngsters from feeder schools who use A.R.R.O.W. in post-school clubs. Support from the parents is such that they undertake the transport of their children to and from the host College. The tutor envisages the further extension of the College facility to adults within the locality.

Chapter 6 Conclusion

There has been recognition of the effectiveness of A.R.R.O.W. in a Dcsf publication. Independent research of A.R.R.O.W. with Year 6 pupils (n=85) at a Bristol Primary School was conducted by the School of Education Exeter University. Results showed a marked improvement in Reading (Word Recognition), Spelling and Comprehension Skills after 10 hours A.R.R.O.W. which was delivered 1 hour per day for 2 weeks. Pupils' comments were positive. A non-A.R.R.O.W. Self-Voice study was also initiated by Exeter University. Extensive use of 1:1 interventions (n=159) were conducted in an experiment which required pupils to listen to themselves reading lists of words. The experiment showed that pupils listening to Self-Voice tasks scored higher on word recognition tasks than groups who did not, including a group who listened to an adult voice when reading their word list. A.R.R.O.W. Self-Voice evidence is presented from 779 pupils attending 35 Primary Schools in Eire, England, Wales, Trinidad and Tobago. Average age was 10+ years with an average reading deficit of 15 months and an average spelling deficit of 18 months. After maximum 10 hour intervention programs, improvements were 9 months reading and 5 months spelling. Two Wigan and one Bolton Primary Schools assessed 27 yr. 1+2 pupils and found they effected improvements averaging 10 months reading and 6 months spelling after 6+ hours. A Year 6 group of 23 pupils from a Devon Primary School undertook an A.R.R.O.W. 2-3 hour intervention program of 30 minutes per day. Reading and spelling standards were 12 months and 18 months respectively below the pupils' average chronological age. Work was differentiated. Results showed an average improvement of 6 months for reading and 4 months for spelling. A spelling control group from the same class showed no upward score movement. Additional Reading, Comprehension, Reading Rate and Spelling assessments were made by the staff and revealed further progress. Students showed high ranking of the Self-Voice method on an Attitude Test. Students for whom English was an additional language at home realised marked improvements. A Leicester Project is described in which a clear ascendancy of A.R.R.O.W. pupils was established when compared to a control group from the same class. Thirty Year 6 Primary School pupils in Lancashire, of average and above average ability, undertook A.R.R.O.W. for a total of 2-3 hours across 3-4 consecutive days. Results showed improvements of at least 8 months for word attack skills and 4 months for spelling skills. Pupils of high ability for reading and spelling based in a Rhondda Valley Primary realised 29 months reading gain and 14 months spelling gain after 10 hours. Secondary Schools/College results taken from 428 students in 19 separate sites. Average reading improvements realise an 8 months upward shift, whilst spelling progress show a 5 months shift. A South West Community College showed 9 months improvement for reading and

4 months improvement for spelling after 2-3 hours A.R.R.O.W. Self-Voice work delivered within one week.

Chapter 7
The Flexibility of A.R.R.O.W.

The West Indies Pattern 84

Eire 85

Distance Learning 86

Case Study 1 86

Case Study 2 87
       Results 88

A Distance Learning Parent from Ireland, writes: 88

Religious Group 89

Important Considerations 89

Tutor Training Procedures 89
       Results Gained 90

An Adult Distance A.R.R.O.W. Program USA 90

Adult Distance A.R.R.O.W. Program UK 91

Chapter 7 Conclusion 93

Chapter 7
The Flexibility of A.R.R.O.W.

This chapter will look at the manner in which A.R.R.O.W. Self-Voice is undertaken by students in a delivery pattern outside the remit usually followed in mainstream schools in the UK and Ireland.

It has been found that A.R.R.O.W. has great flexibility and can be applied in many different ways, although its overall success is undoubtedly dependant upon the pupils completing a required quantity of work. Time on A.R.R.O.W. is usually between 3-8 hours. How this amount of time is organised is up to each and every school and several different formats are being followed. The organisation of A.R.R.O.W. tutors will also vary from site to site and include daily lessons, several lessons per week, weekly lessons, Distance Learning Programs and intensive single session training conducted within 2+ hours.

The West Indies Pattern

Following successful trials in Hertfordshire by Jan Houston, (1997- 2002) a most interesting development has taken place in Trinidad - West Indies, under the leadership of Cornelia Bonterre, a highly regarded A.R.R.O.W. tutor. Here a different, yet equally successful approach to A.R.R.O.W. has been applied for several years. Trained A.R.R.O.W. tutors visit schools, taking all the laptops and materials with them for a prescribed period of time, usually 2-3 weeks. The tutors conduct assessments and work for a period of approximately 8 hours per group of students across 2-4 weeks, before moving on to the next site. Results have been extremely encouraging.

Low literacy skill students at one particular West Indies school showed a marked upward shift of between 3-7 months progress in reading and spelling. Means for pre-intervention reading were 19.3 realising a reading age of 7 years 3 months for 9 year old pupils, i.e. virtually a 2 year deficit against their chronological age. After A.R.R.O.W. the mean rose to 24 showing an improvement of 3 months.

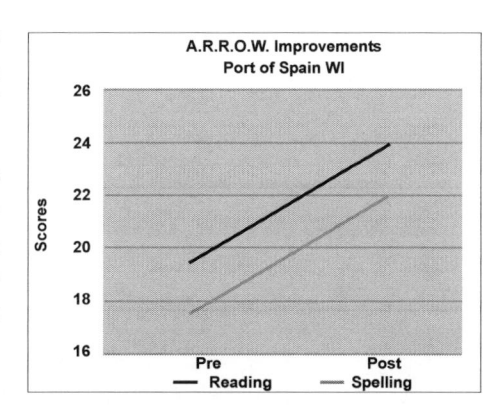

Means for pre-intervention spelling

realised 17.37 a spelling age of 6 years 8 months for 9-year-old pupils i.e. a deficit of 2 years 4 months against their chronological age. After A.R.R.O.W. the mean rose to 22, showing an improvement of 7 months.

A Port of Spain Head Teacher:
"A real eye opener. The children are more aware and want to read. It has whet their appetite and they want more. The children have begun to want to move up in their reading levels and they are gaining independence in their reading. The children now know that they can read, their confidence is continuing to improve and they are initiating their own reading groups." Kathleen Holder, Principal St. David's R.C. Chandernagore Trinidad.

An investigation was also made in Trinidad of the effects of 3 hour A.R.R.O.W. training upon high ability standard 3 and 4 children. No such 2-3 hour investigation had previously been undertaken with this age group. The results reveal a most marked upward movement in performance after less than 3 hours with students of above average ability.

Pre-A.R.R.O.W. average reading scores rose from 66.6 to 77.5 showing a 16 month improvement in word attack skills with standard 3 and 4 children already shown to be above average. Spelling levels also rose sharply, scores moving from an average 55.5 to 58.8 showing a spelling improvement of 4 months across the 6 hour program. One 10 year old child was shown to have made a 23 month shift in reading skills within one hour of commencing the A.R.R.O.W. program. The Head of the School and several other persons witnessed this remarkable progress, a world first for Trinidad.

Another Principal Comments:
"...From the pre and post tests, I found the results remarkable and if this is the extent it can improve our children in a short space of time, I definitely would recommend it." Kitty Garcia La Puerta School Trinidad.

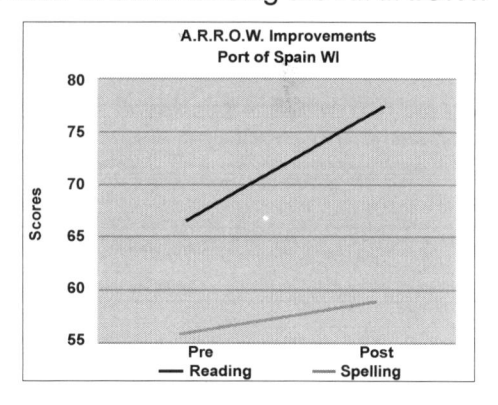

Eire
Two A.R.R.O.W. initiatives were conducted in Southern Ireland between 2009/10. The first initiative was headed by a NEPS regional psychological service under the guidance of Dr. Mary Nugent. Initially six Primary/Secondary age schools in Eire were trained and results were very encouraging. Irish teachers have proven most efficient at implementing A.R.R.O.W. and a tutor trainer has been appointed from amongst the first group of tutors. From the original cohort of 6 schools many more are now implementing A.R.R.O.W. A suggestion by one of the original Irish tutors on extending the Personal Spelling Profile approach to Advanced Spellings has been adopted most successfully.

A second initiative involved the National Behaviour Support Service under the guidance of Mary Keene and has investigated A.R.R.O.W. with the following:

- Students experiencing behaviour problems
- Students at risk of behaviour difficulties because of poor literacy standards

Twenty teachers from 8 selected schools were trained in A.R.R.O.W. and have helped 90+ students taught either in specially selected groups, 1:1 for those requiring individual help, or within a small A.R.R.O.W. group operating amongst a collection of others. The students have averaged 8 months reading improvement and 6 months spelling across 10 hours. These results are most rewarding and are equivalent to those gained by mainstream pupils who do not experience behaviour problems. The students evaluations of the help given by A.R.R.O.W. a category of 'Good' for enjoyment, reading and spelling, are also heartening and parallel many mainstream students views.

Distance Learning
The computer driven facility has greatly enhanced the support available to students of all ages and abilities who cannot access A.R.R.O.W. at a school or college.

Students from Russia, Italy, Spain, and throughout the UK have used the program at home with parental overviewing support. A.R.R.O.W. Distance Learning work allocation is usually 20 minutes per day 4-5 days a week for approximately five weeks. Three to four visits are made to the A.R.R.O.W. centre in order to complete a full program. The first visit is for purposes of assessing the student, designating the specific customised programs on the DVD and training the student and parent in the use of the system. As part of the assessment the child is given a selection of tests exploring lateral dominance, reading, spelling, short term memory, self-esteem and listening skills.

The second visit, usually after a two month period, is for re-testing the student and setting up a new program. The new program is normally resumed after a 3-4 week break from A.R.R.O.W.

Case Study 1
Sandra attended the centre as a Year 6 student in a Birmingham Primary School. Sandra fell within the normal mainstream population and did not require any Special Needs provision. Parents were concerned that she was given every opportunity to reach her potential and hoped she would be able to qualify for placement at a selective Grammar School, as did her brother. School however, did not feel she had the ability for this selective placement, but because of her average attainments at school, could not offer any additional support.

Chapter 7 - The Flexibility of A.R.R.O.W.

At the A.R.R.O.W. Centre, an initial assessment and Distance Learning training were effected. Sandra attended for 3 assessment and program planning sessions spread across 6 months. Her first re-visit to the Centre was after 6-7 weeks. A second and third revisit followed.

Sandra's A.R.R.O.W. work allocation was a prescribed 20 minutes per day 4-5 days a week. Results showed a marked improvement in literacy skills including far greater confidence and ability to read aloud within her class. Mother reported that Sandra would willingly undertake her A.R.R.O.W. work prior to breakfast every morning, thus leaving weekends free for leisure activities.

Date	Reading Pre	Reading Post	Gain Months	Spelling Pre	Spelling Post	Gain Months
31.10.03 3.6.04	41	58	15	50	60	12
10.11.04	58	73	17	60	65	6

"We turned to A.R.R.O.W. because Sandra's teachers had raised concerns over her reading but were unable to help at school because she didn't fall into Special Needs category. The improvement we have seen in just one visit has convinced us that we made the correct choice. Sandra's reading and spelling has shown such a measurable improvement and more importantly her confidence and fluency in group reading has grown. Sandra now has the opportunity to reach her potential as she continues through the A.R.R.O.W. scheme – this is a right every child should have. She needs no prompting to complete the tasks and enjoys the laptop independence. Certainly well motivated enough to manage her A.R.R.O.W. work before the school day".

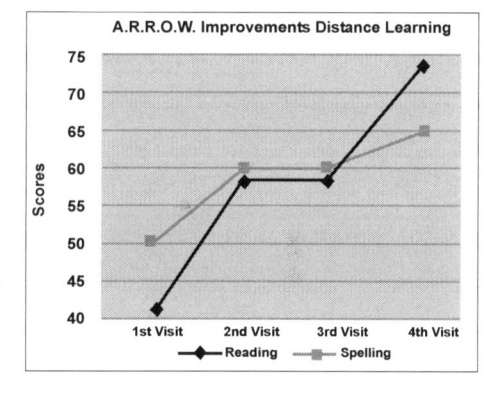

The end result for Sandra was extremely satisfactory. She took the scholarship examination and passed. She now attends one of the most highly regarded schools in the UK.

Case Study 2

Rossano attended an English speaking school in Milan, where he was felt to be extremely shy and retiring. Both parents attended the initial assessment where it was shown that Rossano had a pronounced literacy problem.

Results

Date	Reading Pre	Reading Post	Gain Months	Spelling Pre	Spelling Post	Gain Months
4.9.07 30.10.07	28	50	21	20	31	13

The results after A.R.R.O.W. were, of course, extremely encouraging and both school and parents commented upon the rapid and sustained improvement in Rossano's English work. As a result of the progress made, Rossano's mother received an extended parent awareness training program which paralleled the mainstream tutor training program in use in the UK and elsewhere. Mother therefore, is now able to both assess and monitor Rossano herself without further recourse to the A.R.R.O.W. Centre.

A Distance Learning Parent from Ireland, writes:

"…On a separate note, my own daughter Ellen is 7 weeks into her 1st A.R.R.O.W. intervention. We had the parent/teacher meetings last night and guess what……….??? Both her teacher and her reading support teacher are so impressed by her rapid recent improvement that they feel she no longer needs reading support! I wonder what may have caused that? Needless to say we are absolutely thrilled. Looking forward to meeting up with you at our next opportunity, until then, thanks once more…"

Lesley, another Distance Learning Parent, whose children benefited from A.R.R.O.W. and who later trained to be a tutor writes:

"…just to give you some feedback on the kids who did ARROW with me, My first little girl was nine years old diagnosed with Dyslexia when tested reading and spelling at age 7.7, she did ARROW for four hours, 45 to 50 minute sessions, five days over two weeks, her improvement was astounding, not only did her scores improve incredibly and to the delight of her parents her word attack skills took off she grew in confidence and lost the fear of having a go, which was a feature of her school day. She herself enjoyed ARROW and would like to do more… The next interesting case was a boy eleven years old, when tested reading 8.1, spelling 8.2, having great difficulty in school with Dyslexia, when I met him. He was the boy who didn't like to make eye contact, my impression was he lacked confidence, once he experienced the freedom of ARROW, he made it his own, he enjoyed that he was in charge of his work and he was in control. He did ARROW for 3 hours 20 minutes, over three sessions as he had a long distance to travel weekly. Well, when he finished he was like 'The cat who got the cream', he knew he had done very well, his wide smile said it all, he could do it and he knew it, and yes Colin he wants more. His score improved, reading 9.1 (12 months progress), spelling 8.9 (7 months progress)."
Lesley.

A parent in the UK, Joy Speed, Dyslexic, first used the approach with herself then with her daughter. She states:

"It gave Rebecca much more confidence and her spelling improved tremendously enabling her to get excellent GCSE results. I have myself progressed from typing very slowly, with numerous errors to being able to take dictation with minimal spelling mistakes and it has also helped improve my attention/listening to the point where my husband has noticed a difference!"

Joy has since supported A.R.R.O.W. immeasurably during her role as Company Secretary.

Religious Group

A group of parents, used A.R.R.O.W. for several years within their community. The decision to use A.R.R.O.W. was taken after a member of the group took her child to an A.R.R.O.W. Centre and noted the considerable progress made. The community covered all countries in the UK and Eire and had established their own Secondary Schools outside mainstream education. Discussions were held and an A.R.R.O.W. learning strategy was implemented as follows:

Selected volunteers from within the group became A.R.R.O.W. tutors. Each tutor was responsible for a student(s) attending one of the group's schools. The tutor would attend each school on a Distance Learning basis every four to six weeks. All student assessments and program settings were therefore, the sole responsibility of the trained A.R.R.O.W. tutor.

Important Considerations

The use of computers was new to all the group's personnel as the volunteers were mostly mature adults with no previous IT experience. This meant that the training program would have to include an 'introduction to computers' as part of the general A.R.R.O.W. Tutor Training course. Most of the volunteers were unfamiliar with producing reports, particularly in typed format and would either be using typewriters, or word processors in the absence of computer technology.

It was most illuminating and encouraging that the tutors achieved most positive results with their students despite several apparently severe obstacles:

- Tutors had no previous experience of computers
- The tutors were not trained teachers
- The tutors had no background knowledge of the educational establishments which they visited
- The distance many of the tutors were from their students meant that most visits were 1-2 months apart
- Tutors had virtually no experience in producing the required report at the close of the training program

Tutor Training Procedures

Training for the prospective tutors required travelling throughout the UK to a central training venue for the required training program. The training program was consequently presented on consecutive days on a back-to-back basis. All previous A.R.R.O.W. training programs had intervals between each training day, but because of the travelling constraints, this was no longer possible for this group. The back-to-back formula, conducted on-site, at an educational establishment, was later adopted as standard procedure as a result of:

- The advantages of having children available for demonstration purposes
- Economic and social circumstances which demanded that trainee tutors, many of whom had Teaching Assistant status, could not be expected to travel lengthy distances with the possibility of overnight stays away from families etc.
- Links with specialist IT personnel at a school were best made face to face

It was decided that the A.R.R.O.W. Tutors would assess each student and place them on the appropriate A.R.R.O.W. program. The program was then under the control of an A.R.R.O.W. Overviewing Assistant based in each school. The Overviewing Assistants were given a one-day training program in which they learnt of the general background to A.R.R.O.W., the spelling and reading requirements of the system and how to check each student's progress. The A.R.R.O.W. Tutors ensured that the Overviewing Assistants kept the children on task in terms of work ethic and performance and liaised with them by telephone and during each bi-monthly visit. The overviewing assistant's role was virtually that of a Distance Learning parent.

Results Gained

No students	Average Age	Reading Pre	Reading Post	Gain Months	Spell Pre	Spell Post	Gain Months
9	13.7	67.46	76.6	15	52.13	60.26	9

It can be seen that the work was most successful in raising standards of the students undertaking the program. The stringent requirements placed upon the A.R.R.O.W. system did not negatively affect the outcomes gained and it was self-evident that the care and enthusiasm of the tutors was a key factor in the success of the Self-Voice program.

An Adult Distance A.R.R.O.W. Program USA
The following text was taken from an audio cassette recording forwarded to the author during 2002 by Mrs Barbara Parkes, a widely experienced A.R.R.O.W. tutor. Mrs Parkes travelled to Pennsylvania where she met a distant relative Thomas, who was experiencing severe Dyslexia and was consequently virtually unable to read. Mrs Parkes took an A.R.R.O.W. audio cassette recorder and appropriate level Topic and Spelling books. Mrs Parkes conducted an initial assessment and worked for 3 days, testing and recording Thomas' voice from the A.R.R.O.W. reading and spelling text books. Mrs Parkes in fact, recorded

many weeks work inside the 3 day period. Thomas was then shown how to operate the system and began the A.R.R.O.W. program. Mrs Parkes returned to the UK for several months before returning once again to Pennsylvania. Thomas had worked diligently through the scheme during her absence. The success of the strategy can be gauged from his comments which were recorded and forwarded to the author in the UK.

This is a message for Dr Colin Lane.
"This is Thomas ... 36 years old. I live in the United States. This method I've been working with it really seems to work for me. I've never had the chance for anything like this. I've had other teachers who'd done this, that and the other and nothing seems to have grabbed hold. It is all just slipping by. I've been a life without reading, I'm 36 years old and I'm actually just starting to learn to read. When Mrs Parkes came over in the summer she knew about me, but never talked to me about anything, so I wasn't sure about trying this, but I went ahead and did it anyway and it really has opened my mind to think what I've lost and now what I'm going to gain from your research. I also found out that if you listen to your own voice it makes a big difference and its very important. I'm finally glad that I'm learning to read because it's something I have always needed. I have five children, they always wanted me to read books to them and I've kinda shied away from them but now thanks to this method I've actually read a book to my son finally and hopefully by 6, 7, 8 months from now I can read a lot of books to him. So I'm very grateful that you came up with this method and maybe some day I can read you something and I'm very grateful that you did this. Thank you, and if you were here now I would be very glad to shake your hand, for coming up with this great method to learn to read. I thank you very much."

In the case of Thomas, the pacing and checking of work undertaken in the absence of a tutor required maturity, focus and application. The comments of Thomas however, show that the core elements of A.R.R.O.W. notably the Self-Voice and follow up work undertaken through dictation and self-checking, influenced his progress as much as the undoubted skill and experience of a most respected A.R.R.O.W. tutor. Barbara Parkes, was of course, thousands of miles away in England, when the great majority of the work was being undertaken.

Adult Distance A.R.R.O.W. Program UK
Another exciting example of the power and guiding influence of A.R.R.O.W., Self-Voice is taken from a recording made by Paul, who was descended from the famous Victorian author Charles Dickens. Paul initially attended A.R.R.O.W. with minimal reading skills and received help from Ruth, a volunteer, who trained as an A.R.R.O.W. Tutor. Her patience and empathy with her adult students was immeasurable. Ruth saw Paul once weekly and helped record his voice and set up work programs for him at home. Paul's first reading program was at a very elementary 5-6 word level yet he made highly commendable progress after five weeks of A.R.R.O.W. Paul undertook follow-up work at home, listening to his own voice, taking dictation and marking his writing from

graded work programs. His first topic was at an almost pre-reading level.

The Red Bus
I like the red bus.
The red bus is big.
The red bus goes fast.
The red bus goes to town.

1. What do I like?
2. What is big?
3. What goes fast?
4. Where does the red bus go?

Ruth's task was to record as much material as she felt necessary for Paul to attempt at home. Paul took several hours A.R.R.O.W. homework each week and had his progress checked on his return to the centre. It became apparent to the author that Paul was totally committed to improving his reading and was already making quite remarkable progress through the graded reading/spelling programs.

This is a transcript of a recording the author made with Paul after his first five week intervention.

"My name's Paul Dickens…my age is 44, I am descended from a famous Victorian author. A.R.R.O.W. helps me to pronounce words and helps me to read better. I do my recording at Bridgwater at A.R.R.O.W. I take my recording home and do my homework at home.

I've been coming five weeks. When I was little I had meningitis and it held me up from my work at school and it caused me to have epilepsy and now I am an epileptic…"

"This is Colin Lane who has been overviewing Paul and this morning about three quarters of an hour ago said that one day he would read Charles Dickens own works. I've just popped out to the shops and bought David Copperfield. Paul's reading age had improved eighteen months in five weeks. He is going to read some of David Copperfield for you."

"I record that I was born, as I have been informed and believe on Friday at twelve o'clock at night, it was remarked that the clock began to strike and I began to cry simultaneously. In consideration at the day and hour of my birth it was declared by the nurse and by…"

Paul's reading went from strength to strength, he became an avid reader and he was finally able to research, through books, his great love of ships. When the author last saw Paul he was proud to reveal his knowledge of the S.S. Titanic, gained through his greatly improved reading skills. Sadly, Paul acquired a terminal cancer and died a few months later, yet his belief in the progress he had made and the power given to him through reading, remained right to the end of his days. It is a lesson those of us privileged to know Paul Dickens will never forget.

Chapter 7 Conclusion
The great flexibility of A.R.R.O.W. is evident from work conducted under various conditions and across several countries. Success greatly relies upon a pupil completing a requisite amount of work, usually undertaken in 3-8 hours. In Trinidad, tutors trained in A.R.R.O.W. take DVD material, laptops and expertise into schools for several weeks before moving on. Results are impressive. A school with a reading deficit of 2 years and a spelling deficit of 2 yrs. 4 months averaged a 7 month improvement in both reading and spelling skills following A.R.R.O.W. A Port of Spain Headteacher comments most favourably on the improvement of reading (16 months) and spelling skills (4 months) with her above average pupils. Some students have been taking Distance Learning programs in which they firstly attend the A.R.R.O.W. Centre. The students receive literacy, Short Term Memory and listening assessments and afterwards are allocated appropriate reading and spelling programs for later use at home. A.R.R.O.W. is loaded onto a laptop computer and both pupil and parent(s) are familiarised with the approach before taking the materials away. An example is given of a female pupil aged 10+ years who after two visits to A.R.R.O.W. undertaken across 6 months, completed follow-up work at home and made 32 months progress in reading and 18 months progress in spelling. A second example reveals that an Italian boy attending an English school in Italy gained 21 months reading and 13 months spelling after a Distance Learning Program. A parent upgraded her Distance Learning training and became an A.R.R.O.W. Tutor where she achieved considerable success with her first cohort of pupils. A group of volunteers undertook A.R.R.O.W. tuition with Secondary Age pupils. The volunteers were completely inexperienced in the use of computers, but nevertheless, made marked progress with their students. Tutor training procedures were laid down which included computer familiarisation and the introduction of a two day back-to-back training schedule. A Distance Learning set of schedules were adopted in which the tutors assessed the students, then left the laptops and programs at each child's school under the care of an Overviewing Assistant, who in effect undertook the role of a Distance Learning parent. The visiting A.R.R.O.W. Tutor made regular six weekly assessments of progress. Adults have most successfully undertaken A.R.R.O.W. Distance Learning. A 36 year old father from Pennsylvania was left with Self-Voice work programs by a trained A.R.R.O.W. Tutor visiting the United States. Following an initial assessment and recording of appropriate programs, the adult worked alone for two months and showed that he had made great progress. A trained volunteer at the A.R.R.O.W. Centre worked on a weekly basis with an adult with severe literacy problems. The adult improved his reading and spelling skills to such an extent that he moved from being a low ability reader to one in which he could adequately attempt to read a passage from Charles Dicken's 'David Copperfield'.

Chapter 8
A.R.R.O.W. in the Community

Exploratory Work 97

Adults with Stroke – An Introduction 97

Adults Within an Ageing Population – An Introduction 98

Adults with Alzheimer's 99

Adult with Severe Learning Problems – An Introduction 100

Meningitis 101

Adult with Traumatic Brain Injury – An Introduction 102

Adult with Autism - An Introduction 102

A Summary of Common Core Problems for Adults with Literacy
and Speech/Communication Needs 103

Ground Breaking 104

The Bridgwater College 'Your Skills' A.R.R.O.W. Course 104

A.R.R.O.W. Tutors 104

Delivery of A.R.R.O.W. 105

The 'Your Skills' A.R.R.O.W. Program Contents: 105

Comprehension 105

Free Writing Following Self-Voice Dictation 105

Survival Words 105

Spellings 105

Four Key Questions 105

Community Groups 106

Differentiation and Score Measurement 106

Group 1, Adults with CVA Stroke 106

    Stroke N = 39 1st Intervention 107
    Stroke N = 30 2nd Intervention 107
    The Effects of Further Interventions 107
    Case Study 108
    Mrs Margaret Thomas Heather Stroke Club Organiser, Bridgwater .. 110
    Lynda Parkinson, at the time, Organiser Burnham and Highbridge
    Stroke Club 110
    Louise Greswell, Speech and Language Therapist when helping
    Adults with Stroke 111
    Comments by Adults 111

A.R.R.O.W. Your Skills Interventions - Group 2, Adults in
Residential Homes 111
    Residential Homes N = 30   1st Intervention 112
    Residential Homes N = 19   2nd Intervention 112

Group 3, Adults with Severe Learning Problems 115
    General Background 115
    Learning Problem Adults 115
    Learning Problem Adults 1st Intervention 115
    Learning Problem Adults 2nd Intervention 115

A.R.R.O.W. Your Skills Interventions - Group 4, Headway - Adults
with Brain Injury 117
    Results discussed 118

Testimonials 119

Chapter 8 Conclusion 119

Chapter 8
A.R.R.O.W. in the Community

A.R.R.O.W. has helped adults in the community who have learning and/or communication problems. In essence, the 1978-80 research project with school pupils with listening and speech disorders, led the way for further work with adults with communication difficulties. After successful trials, first initiated by Steve Trelfa, Bridgwater College, in association with A.R.R.O.W., established a 'Your Skills' course in Plymouth, Devon and Somerset and Bristol which was instrumental in helping to extend the technique into the adult sector. Seven Bridgwater College tutors were trained in A.R.R.O.W. The tutors covered a catchment area over 150 miles long which extended from Plymouth, Devon, Dorset to North Somerset and Bristol. Some 200 adults per year were helped by A.R.R.O.W. tutors at Stroke Clubs, Residential Homes, Learning Centres or Centres for Adults with Brain Injury. Let us see how this innovative A.R.R.O.W. Self-Voice work first developed in the adult sector and the nature of the results it has achieved.

Exploratory Work
During the early beginnings of A.R.R.O.W. and until the late 1980's, little was known of the effects of A.R.R.O.W. type Self-Voice work with adults with learning and/or communication problems. In 1987, visits were made by the author to investigate the viability of A.R.R.O.W. with this non-school, older population.

Adults with Stroke – An Introduction
Over 130,000 people per year have a stroke in England and Wales and it is estimated that there are currently over 450,000 people in England alone, living with severe disability as the result of a stroke. Stroke is due to disturbance in the brain's blood supply, the result of a blocked or burst blood vessel. Results of stroke can be inhibition of movement of one or both limbs, speech and understanding of speech and/or inability to see one side or more of visual field.

Some victims of Stroke have been informed that interventions would be unsuccessful if conducted several years after the incidence of stroke and/or early rehabilitation techniques had ceased. A.R.R.O.W. found evidence to the contrary. A most interesting point is, how did A.R.R.O.W. enter this adult field when all previous Self-Voice work had been with school age students?

A visit was made in 1987, to a former senior educational advisor who had supported the use of A.R.R.O.W. with Hearing Impaired children. He had, since his retirement, experienced the effects of a stroke which had left him with severe Aphasia. He agreed to the visit in order to explore whether A.R.R.O.W. would hold any benefit for him. The adult was able, with help from the tutor, to read and record a few lines of text from Cornelius Ryan's book 'The Longest

Day'. The intention was for him to try and follow his own recording and also gauge his reaction to hearing himself on Self-Voice playback. When the A.R.R.O.W. recording was being replayed, the adult, unprompted, smiled upon hearing his own voice. He confirmed that the use of Split Record was very beneficial to him in helping construct the appropriate language structure from the text. From this point on, and as far as he was able, he proved a continual source of encouragement in the work.

In 1999, a one week experiment was initiated at Liverpool Dysphasia Support Group. The adults attended the University Hospital Aintree for a maximum of 2 hours per day across a 5 day intervention program. Two trained A.R.R.O.W. tutors, assisted by volunteer support staff, delivered the program to groups of no more than 4 adults at a time. A characteristic of the program was the highly individual nature of requirements for each student. One group was offered literacy training, another group undertook listening training, whilst a third group received speech training programs. A battery of 5 tests were administered to those adults able to undertake the assessments based upon viz. Word Understanding, Word Reading, Spelling and Short Term Memory for Digits/ Words.

Word Understanding Scores rose from an average of 18 to 41 within the one week program, an improvement of 127%. Word Recognition scores showed an average improvement of 20% across the 10 hour program. Spelling scores realised a 24% average improvement, whilst Digit and Word Recall scores improved by 22% and 36% respectively.

It was observed on several occasions that the adults with stroke both smiled and silently mouthed when listening to their own replayed voices and many clients self-checked their speech when producing words or individual phonemes during recordings. The impact of A.R.R.O.W. with the group was best summarised by one adult who was heard to say to himself, *"Oh my hat, I can read again"*.

Adults Within an Ageing Population – An Introduction

There has been a massive rise in the elderly population since the beginning of the 20th century. In 1901, the UK population of 65-84 year olds was estimated at 1.7 million, by 1961 it had risen to 5.8 million, by 1991 it had risen to 8.2 million, and by 2011 was to have reached 8.7 million, five times the 1901 population. This development has meant a concomitant rise in the need for care of the elderly particularly in residential homes. It is usually accepted that declining age is characterised by a fall-off in learning performances. There was in fact, exploratory work, conducted by the author, in the late 1980's, involving Self-Voice work with elderly adults with a hearing loss. There has been however, very little Self-Voice research with the generic elderly population as a whole, particularly when based within residential homes and it was indeed fortunate that the opportunity arose to explore this avenue.

Adults with Alzheimer's

Alzheimer's Disease is the most common form of dementia and is at present defined as an incurable, degenerative, and terminal disease. Generally, it is diagnosed in people over 65 years of age, although early-onset Alzheimer's can occur before this. An estimated 26.6 million people worldwide had Alzheimer's in 2006 and it is possible that this number may quadruple by 2050. Alzheimer's is characterised by communication, memory and personality problems. Treatments to delay or halt the progression are under surveillance and research indicates that the disease is associated with plaques and tangles in the brain. Mental stimulation, exercise and a balanced diet are suggested as a possible prevention and a sensible way of managing the illness.

The first A.R.R.O.W. Self-Voice work with an adult suffering from Alzheimer's, was conducted in 1990. A request was made by a former teaching friend to see whether A.R.R.O.W. could help her 60 year old husband John, who was suffering from the debilitating disease. A small experiment was set up at his home. The author asked John to sit alongside and listen to him reading aloud a short passage about the Grand Canyon. Whilst the author was reading aloud, John was trying to silently read the text from the book containing the passage. He was then asked to write down answers based upon simple questions. The original text and questions based upon this are given below.

The Grand Canyon
A canyon is a steep and narrow place. There is a very big canyon in America. It is called The Grand Canyon. The Grand Canyon is millions of years old. There is a river at the bottom of it. The canyon is two hundred miles long. In some parts it is a mile deep. A tribe of Indians live in the canyon. There are many kinds of birds and animals who live there. Some of the animals are snakes and lizards.

1. What is a canyon?
2. Where is the Grand Canyon?
3. How long is the Grand Canyon?
4. How old is the Grand Canyon?
5. Who lives in the Grand Canyon?
6. Which animals live in the Grand Canyon?

His written responses after first listening to the author reading aloud, were as follows:

A canna is
Seven 5 miles
It is very li
5 Burrows who live in the sides
Total words written: 17.

John then recorded the same passage using A.R.R.O.W. and listened back to his Self-Voice recording whilst following the same material from the book. His responses to the identical questions spoken again by the author, after Self-Voice listening, were as follows:

A canyon
The canyon is a steep and narrow place
In our America
May
That canay is a his millions old
200 uners long
The tribe of Indians live the canyon
Some of the animals live our snakes and lizards, porcupines if others bea and
Total words written: 45, with a far greater accuracy of response than previously.

John also undertook a ten word spelling test based upon the following words. about, cat, hand, has, and, absent, advance, able, cable, table.

His first, pre A.R.R.O.W. responses were
Sp, cat, p, has, and you and I, absent, advance, abable, cable, table. 5 errors.

He was then given 10 minutes A.R.R.O.W. Self-Voice training on the ten words. After a 40 minute delay from the end of training, he was then given the test again. His responses were superior to those given before *'about', 'cat', 'hand', 'has', 'absent', 'advance', 'able', 'cacle', 'cable', 'table'.* 1 error.

An A.R.R.O.W. 'Your Skills' tutor worked in 2003-4 with an adult, Tom, aged 50+ years with recognised Altzheimer's. She reports that when first entering the A.R.R.O.W. program, Tom's total speech output consisted of three sentences with correct intent. These sentences contained swear words which were repeated continually. Word matching exercises were introduced involving Self-Voice replay of single words followed by written reinforcement. A scrabble board was used to extend the word length and include these within sentences which were recorded and replayed back to him using Self-Voice. At the close of the first 10 hour course, he was able to repeat more sentences of increasing length and recall some of these after a few weeks. It should be noted, however, that swearing was maintained in running speech although meaningful vocabulary increased.

Adult with Severe Learning Problems – An Introduction
Educators and employers in the UK report that the number of adults without a satisfactory level of literacy and/or communication skills is quite unacceptable. A Basic Skills Agency Report in 2000, found that nearly 40% of adults could not read or write properly or complete 'simple sums'. In 2003, it was felt that over 5 million adults would fail to pass an English GCSE (National Needs and Impact Survey of Literacy, Numeracy and ICT Skills, DfES October 2003). The causes of severe learning problems are numerous. Socio economic factors, innate intelligence levels, lack of educational opportunities and the effects of various

illnesses can have a direct impact upon literacy standards and communication skills. One of the various illnesses causing severe learning and communication problems, notably Meningitis, resulted in exploratory work with a teenager which had a direct impact upon the further development and application of A.R.R.O.W. learning methodologies with all ages of learners.

Meningitis

As many as 500,000 people living in the UK today have had either viral or bacterial meningitis at some time in their lives. It is anticipated that there are currently some 5,500 persons in the UK suffering from the effects of the illness. Meningitis can lead to many debilitating memory and communication skill deficits, including deafness. A request from a Care Centre Manager led to some very interesting A.R.R.O.W. work and offers hope for sufferers of either the viral or bacterial form of the disease.

Following an attack of meningitis, an adolescent West Country girl, Julie, had lost all working short-term memory. Her ability to communicate was at a non-verbal level. From being a prospective College student, she was placed in a Special Care Centre in Somerset. She had no conversation skills and could not recall any items which had been shown and named for her just seconds before. When listening to the word 'sun', and asked what had been said, she responded with 'table' or other non-relevant words. Split Record and Echoing techniques were employed. The girl heard the word 'sun' spoken by the author. After considerable prompting she copied the tutor's voice saying 'sun' and her recording of 'sun' was echoed back to her. She was asked to point to a hastily drawn symbol of the sun when it was pointed out to her. After several echoes and word identification tasks, using pointing to a symbol of the sun as the required response, she was able to repeat, 'sun'. Later in the session the word 'moon', was introduced using similar techniques. Julie could identify each 'sun', 'moon', symbol provided that the identification task was presented immediately after Echoing of the Self-Voice. In a second session, Julie was able to point to the appropriate words 'sun' and 'moon' in written form.

Two key strategies were employed when requesting further information from Julie during follow-up sessions:

1. Julie was asked, "Show me the word, 'sun' please" and was expected to point to the word 'sun'.
2. Immediately afterwards she was asked, "What does it say?" and had to respond by saying "sun".

Julie successfully completed these tasks and then progressed to a pencil picture of the moon. She again showed that she was able to identify both the picture and the word "moon" following rapid Echoing of her Self-Voice recording of "moon".

The author then wrote individual flash cards making up a short sentence

| I | see | the | sun |

Each word was recorded individually using Split Record techniques. The four word sentence was played back in its entirety. Julie was asked, "Show me the word 'I' and was immediately asked "What does it say?". After correctly speaking, "I", she was asked to follow the same procedures for the remaining words, 'see', 'the', 'sun'. Julie showed she could achieve these targets. The Self-Voice sentence was then played again in its entirety and Julie was able to repeat all four words correctly. In a later session, Julie was able to identify the words when presented in random order after Self-Voice Echoing. She was then able to place the words in the correct sequence.

The Head of the Care Centre attended the A.R.R.O.W. session with Julie and based upon her observations, decided to undertake the Tutor Training course. She worked with Julie herself on the early level programs. After twelve months, sufficient communication and literacy skill progress had been made for Julie to enrol on a Basic Skills course at Bridgwater College and she began to mix once again with a peer group of students.

Adult with Traumatic Brain Injury – An Introduction
It is estimated that across the UK there are around 500,000 people aged between 16–74 years, living with long term disabilities as a result of traumatic brain injury. The effects can be devastating in terms of changing life style, communication skills, academic achievement and patterns of mobility.

Bill, was a 21 year old adult who was comatose after a car crash left him with severe head injuries. Mother reported that a succession of specialists tried in vain to help him following the car crash. She requested help for Bill from The A.R.R.O.W. Centre. When conducting the initial interview, it was found that Bill's interest was cars. In order to speed up Bill's speech, which tended to be laborious and a monotone, he practised passages of information about cars. Initially, the recordings were made in a very slow fashion but then were recorded with an increasingly faster speed of delivery. Bill practised A.R.R.O.W. at home. After several weeks there was a marked improvement not only in his practised material, but in his everyday speech.

Bill said:
"It's opened up a whole new world for me. My speech is so much better than before. I'm not saying I was ever a great singer and after the accident it was difficult for me to even hum a note. I became very inward looking, lonely and shy when I talked to girls and got a sympathetic smile. I get a genuine one as long as I say something funny of course. It's brilliant."

Adult with Autism - An Introduction
The National Autistic Society give estimates for Autism. The figure for children is based on the 1 in 100 prevalence rate and estimates suggest that some

133,500 children under 18 years fall within the Autistic Spectrum Disorder (ASD). Given that there is no prevalence rate for ASD in adults, the figure for the whole population is a very rough guide, but it is estimated that there could be over 500,000 people who fall within the Autistic Spectrum Disorder category.

One of the adults who met A.R.R.O.W. at a residential centre, was classified as within the ASD spectrum. David was in his mid twenties. He had few social skills in terms of interacting with others and was very satisfied to occupy his time in producing repetitive artistic drawings and/or patterns of a bizarre nature. His comprehension skills upon reading a passage, graded according to his reading ability, were non-existent.

After a few months basic A.R.R.O.W., he was observed to read a sign, 'EXIT' and say aloud, *"Exit, that means way out"*. Later he was able to extract meaning from Topics he had read. Upon reading a topic based upon 'The Romans in Britain', the author asked him:

Q   "David, what is a milecastle?" and responded
A   *"It's like a tower"*
Q   "How far apart were they?"
A   *"Oh, they were placed a mile apart."*
Q   "How far is a mile?"
A   *"It's over there a long way."*

Visits to other adults at the South Wales centre, who also had learning and/or psychological problems, indicated to officers involved in their care, that the use of A.R.R.O.W. Self-Voice methods, particularly the use of Echoing and Split Record, would be most useful learning strategies to use.

A Summary of Common Core Problems for Adults with Literacy and Speech/Communication Needs

There exists a common core of problems for adults with literacy and communication difficulties. Whilst some of these problems may be physiological in nature, and outside the remit of A.R.R.O.W., there are clearly areas where the Self-Voice system can help.

It is widely know that the following skills can deteriorate for adults with literacy and/or communication problems:

- Speaking and communicating and/or understanding intent of others
- Listening during conversation and also during noisy and stressful environments
- Reading both for pleasure and for information
- Writing
- Working short-term memory, attention and concentration - thinking of words when talking or writing

- Less-than-normal behaviour and personality levels in which anxiety and depression, loss of motivation and difficulty in controlling emotions can emerge
- Relationships with family and friends can be placed under immense strain
- Loss of co-ordination, muscle rigidity, paralysis, epilepsy, loss of sight, smell or taste, fatigue and sexual problems

It will be remembered that the components within the A.R.R.O.W. acronym Aural–Read–Respond–Oral–Write, cover many of the literacy and communication problems classified above. It was intuitively felt by the author that the use of A.R.R.O.W. - based literacy and communication skills, i.e. reading, spelling and writing, would lie within previous school experiences of the adults and help form a familiar working background for both adult and tutor.

Ground Breaking

Given the success of the exploratory work it was decided to further extend the scope of A.R.R.O.W. Bridgwater College and A.R.R.O.W. agreed to work together with the express purpose of taking the Self-Voice technique to adults within West Country communities. It had been shown in 1979-80 how the improvement of the listening and communication skills had been most successfully undertaken with language disordered school-age students. The use of A.R.R.O.W. with adults experiencing communication difficulties, was therefore, not without precedence in terms of Self-Voice training. The work was however, exploring new avenues in terms of the potential age of students, the nature of handicap and effectiveness of the approach. It also asked questions about the use of A.R.R.O.W. Tutors within the community and the learning materials to be employed.

The Bridgwater College 'Your Skills' A.R.R.O.W. Course

The course was of 10 hours duration and was delivered in 1 hour sessions on a 10 week basis. An assessment was made of the adults literacy skills, viz Word Recognition, Spellings, Working Short Term Memory and Listening Skills and additionally included each adult's identification of their own particular areas for improvement. The reading and spelling assessments were designed by the author and closely followed the format of the tests used with the school age mainstream population. It is found that the range of adults' skills varied widely and nine separate programs, each at appropriate levels of ability and content, were designed to cover the extensive range of literacy and communication programs required.

A.R.R.O.W. Tutors

A.R.R.O.W. tutors delivering the 'Your Skills' course were initially selected on the basis of having empathy, management skills and a clear commitment to helping adults with communication difficulties. Most tutors undertook the standard A.R.R.O.W. training programs, but submitted reports based on their experiences in the community. A few established tutors had previously worked with school age students but were easily able to transfer and adapt their skills to the adults they met.

Delivery of A.R.R.O.W.

A.R.R.O.W. was delivered on a weekly basis at each site with tutors transporting their materials for use within each session. The adult student and A.R.R.O.W. tutor sat side by side. The adult response was recorded and, if necessary, corrected and replayed to them. The student wrote/typed down, in draft form, from the recorded Self-Voice/text link. The tutor corrected the work so that the student was then able to re-write/type it verbatim and could take it away for reinforcement and revision at home.

The 'Your Skills' A.R.R.O.W. Program Contents:

The aim of the course was that students undertake a range of learning activities and achieve success in the following tasks:

Comprehension

Recognise a poster or topics of information which are ability graded according to each adult.
Search for information from maps and graded topics.
Complete forms and applications.

Free Writing Following Self-Voice Dictation

Use Word Attack skills in sentence construction.
Compose three diary entries based upon linguistic complexity.
Write records based upon 'Likes and Dislikes'.
Write letters according to ability levels.

Survival Words

Students should be able to recognise 20 survival words and their use within graded sentences and give verbal, visual and written descriptions of the environment including their learning centre or club, home and world outside.

Spellings

Students meet the standard A.R.R.O.W. procedures based upon word recognition, letter or sound naming and writing. These are graded according to spelling ability. Spellings included within the programs are based upon survival words used within the environment and include examples such as, 'Exit', 'Toilets', 'Library', 'Church', 'Mosque', 'No Entry', 'Bus Station', 'Railway Station'.

Four Key Questions

The community based program posed four major questions:

1. Could adults with speech and learning difficulties improve their literacy, communication and short-term memory skills given A.R.R.O.W intervention?
2. Could any forthcoming improvements be maintained?
3. Could progress be ongoing given a succession of interventions?
4. Would the education-based work programs be appropriate for the post school age population?

Community Groups
The subjects were split into four major groups.

Group 1   Contained adults who were suffering from a cerebral vascular accident or CVA - Stroke.
Group 2   Contained adults who were in residential homes including some with CVA and/or Dementia or Autism.
Group 3   Contained adults with Severe Learning Problems including some whose problems stemmed from Traumatic Brain Injury (TBI) as a result of accidents or other causes.
Group 4   Comprised adults attending Headway Centres for Adults with Brain Injury.

Data is available from each of the previously identified four groups, but it is important to recognise that there may be overlap between the groups themselves as a result of some students having multiple handicaps.

Differentiation and Score Measurement
All four groups accessed the same programs, but worked at various levels according to initial assessment performance and professional judgment of the tutor. Each A.R.R.O.W. component, Aural, Read, Respond, Oral, Write, was stressed according to the need of each student, but has the Self-Voice central to each lesson. Evidence is available from the initial cohort of 39 adults at the two Stroke clubs. Reading and Spelling scores are given as a % of the original score i.e. the difference between the re-test score and the original base line score. Digit and Word Recall scores show the percentage improvements from a maximum score of 100.

Group 1, Adults with CVA Stroke
The interventions took place at various times during a 4 year period 2004-2008. One of the first sites to undertake A.R.R.O.W. was The Heather Club based at Bridgwater, whilst another site was The Burnham and Highbridge Stroke Club. The two Stroke Clubs were voluntary organisations meeting once weekly. Tutoring at both clubs was undertaken in a room which was separate to the members' main activities area. Following an initial filtering by club organisers, a cohort of 39 adults were able to undertake the initial assessment procedures. Some 12 adults were in fact able to successfully follow 6 intervention programs. The Literacy and Communication abilities of the members varied widely, but all responded in a most positive manner to A.R.R.O.W. Self-Voice strategies.

Stroke N = 39 1st Intervention
See appendix 22

The evidence from the initial total population n = 39 shows a marked improvement in both communication and memory skills after the first A.R.R.O.W. intervention.

The following improvements were recorded after 8 lessons of 45 minutes duration:

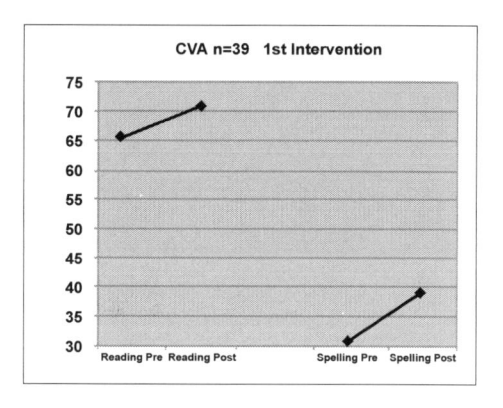

- Reading Skills   8.39%   improvement after 1st intervention
- Spelling Skills   22.91%   improvement after 1st intervention
- Digit Recall   8.95%   improvement after 1st intervention
- Word Recall   13.17%   improvement after 1st intervention

A second intervention was undertaken in which 30 from the original 39 subjects were able to partake in the project. Again, 8 lessons of 45 minutes duration were covered.

Stroke N = 30 2nd Intervention
See appendix 23

- Reading Skills   6.42%   further progress
- Spelling Skills   14.77%   further progress
- Digit Recall   9.4%   further progress
- Word Recall   13.24%   further progress

Evidence again reveals an improvement in Reading, Spelling and Short Term Memory skills. It was shown that:

- Marked progress was again made following the second intervention
- There was no regression to the original scores after a 2-3 month delay between the closure of the first intervention and commencement of the second

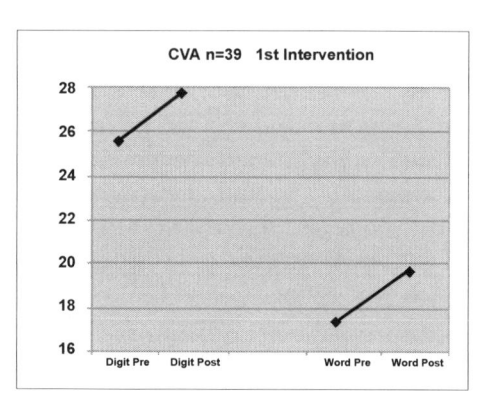

The Effects of Further Interventions
See appendix 24

The rising pattern of improvements continued throughout all interventions. The evidence is provided in the following table based upon data from 12 adults who completed 6 interventions between the years 2004/2006.

- Reading Skills   32.54%   overall improvement
- Spelling Skills   135.84%   overall improvement
- Digit Recall   11.76%   overall improvement
- Word Recall   22.89%   overall improvement

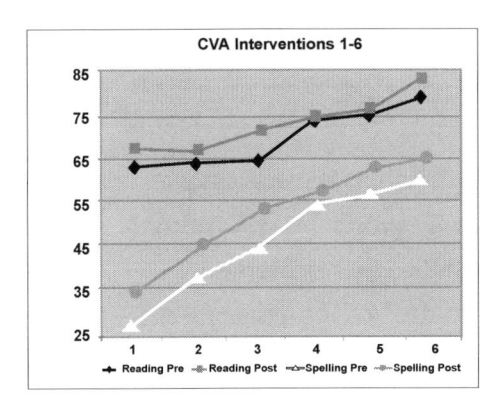

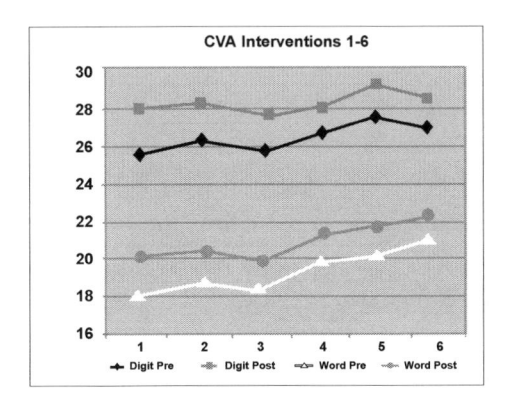

These final results from the selected sample of adults with Stroke show:

- The continuing improvements in literacy and communication skills after six interventions
- The absence of a regression to the base line commencement scores during non-intervention periods
- Improvements in learning processes were obtained several years after the onset of stroke

Case Study
Jim had received a severe stroke some five years before he received A.R.R.O.W. training. Family were informed that he had reached a ceiling in terms of his language and communication skills. He was not capable of spontaneous speech and his usual response to other persons questions or statements was a sometimes unrelated utterance, "All right thank you". It was decided to try to help Jim break this pattern of perseveration by enabling him to experience an increasing number of appropriate Self-Voice responses.

The A.R.R.O.W. Strategies Used with Jim
Split Record and Echoing
Two major strategies were adopted. The first involved the "standard" A.R.R.O.W. format in which Jim was required to repeat two or three word phrases or sentences and then have these replayed back. It was sometimes necessary to use Split Record techniques in order to build up the required Self-Voice speech sample. The speech sample was often linked to text, either available in a graded A.R.R.O.W. book or written by the tutor. Initially, samples of text were limited to repeating one or two word utterances which lay within his

working short term memory. These samples were first introduced by the tutor, then practised with Jim, "live", before attempting to record them after listening to the computer's master recording.

When using the A.R.R.O.W. DVD under tutor guidance, Jim soon showed himself capable of listening to the voice whilst looking at the text, recording, then listening back to the recordings, which he would repeat again after first hearing his own voice. It was interestingly observed that Jim was more readily able to repeat phrases or short sentences when he heard them in his own voice than when he heard them in the Tutor voice. This feature reinforces the view that the mental lexicon finds exposure to the replayed Self-Voice greatly assists speech production and memory recall. It was also found that Jim could anticipate, solely by face reading the first lip shape, word, phrase or sentence he had seen using A.R.R.O.W.

Links to Music

A second, and equally innovative strategy, was asking Jim to repeat, in prose form, songs which he had previously sung and listened to on Self-Voice replay. The rationale behind this tactic was that the 'musicality' of a song sometimes remains within the cortex although other language processing skills have been damaged. It was hoped that Jim would be able to initially sing and record through A.R.R.O.W. a song which would then be replayed to him. Afterwards, the song would be 'spoken out' by Jim and recorded a word, phrase, or sentence at a time, helping build up a bank of accessible spoken language and thereby aiming to open up neural pathways to speech production.

The songs

Jim had once been an enthusiastic singer and songs were based upon the decades in which Jim grew up and included amongst others, 'Run rabbit run', 'I'm forever blowing bubbles', 'I believe' and 'You'll never walk alone'. Jim listened to the voice, and recorded by singing, the phrase or sentence he heard. Jim listened to his recordings and was then asked to repeat the phrase or sentence using normal prose, not his sung version. Using a combination of Split Record techniques linked to text, Jim showed he was quite capable of performing this task and eventually could repeat and speak the text of several songs.

Memory Training Based Upon Life Experiences

Prior to his stroke, Jim had owned a chain of butchers shops in London. Shops were at Camden Town, Finchley, Golders Green, Kentish Town, Muswell Hill and elsewhere in the capital. Following help from the author, Jim had these locations recorded and replayed in his own voice. After practice sessions, he was then able to repeat these locations in sequence. After a few weeks he could repeat most of these without help.

It was decided to see whether a movie based upon pre-stroke experiences would assist Jim's recall of information. The Welsh National Folk Museum at St

Fagans, kindly allowed filming of buildings which lay within the life span of people from Stroke clubs. Amongst these buildings was a prefab built during the 1950's. It was thought that the prefab would form a relevant topic for elderly adults with communication difficulties. Jim followed the standard A.R.R.O.W. approach and was able to listen to himself repeating information relating to the prefab - a building and its rooms which clearly held much meaning for him. He was then able to repeat these in sequence without prompting.

Work at Home

An A.R.R.O.W. DVD program was loaded onto Jim's laptop and his granddaughter undertook follow up training at home – 30 minutes maximum per session, two sessions per week. His granddaughter soon reported that Jim was able to speak material before listening to the tutor recorded voice and was able to read it aloud or speak spontaneously once he recognised the page of text or saw an appropriate movie.

Jim and Kit

Jim's Wife Kit Observed:
"Jim has quite often of late, amazed me by speaking different words I haven't heard since he had his stroke. I'm very pleased by the progress he is making. A.R.R.O.W. has meant that he is saying more."

Mrs Margaret Thomas Heather Stroke Club Organiser, Bridgwater
"While members of the Heather Club were on holiday last week with carers and helpers, many carers said how much your work with them was helping to improve speech and giving them more confidence to try to produce words. Indeed, as a helper, I was surprised at the newfound independence some of them showed, particularly when choosing food and in the case of John even ordering drinks at the bar. Jim amazed everyone by singing along with the evening's entertainments and really producing the words."

Lynda Parkinson, at the time, Organiser Burnham and Highbridge Stroke Club
"In a very short time the club members had improved immensely all due to the hard work and determination from both parties. For instance some can run all their sentences together and for longer periods of time-before they stuttered and babbled. Others whom spoke choose to hear their own voices now quieten down because they are thinking more before talking. Even the one member who could not speak now has a word or two he can say. Marvellous news Colin. But others have a more personal goal and that since having had a stroke they could not write very much and now with the help you have shown can and have written essays and letters which were taboo."

Louise Greswell, Speech and Language Therapist when helping Adults with Stroke

"I write to thank you for the generous amount of time and effort you have spent by the members of West Somerset stroke club.

Mrs. W. in particular has derived an enormous benefit from using A.R.R.O.W. with you. She is now much happier, more self confident and willing to persevere in conversation whereas previously she was depressed, unwilling to try at communicating and severely struggled to make effective communication. I believe that the time you have spent with Mrs. W on A.R.R.O.W. has increased her self awareness of her own voice, fluency and expanding expressive language (vocabulary and grammar use). Self monitoring of her own speech and language has allowed her to generalise new semantic and syntactic constructions, into every day, functional life interactions. She is able to communicate effectively within a semantic grouping of word meanings for names, places and use improved grammar to express word meaning. Her sense of rhythm and intonation use is also improving as is her use of the written word and facial expression to cue verbal expression. Thank you for your help and the increased wellbeing and communication skills Mrs. W has. I wish you well with your project."

Comments by Adults

LF   *"I liked recording my voice. I liked doing computers on my memory and spelling. I was pleased about the course."*

TF   *"I liked the course very much. I have to write and think. I want to do more work on the course."*

A.R.R.O.W. Your Skills Interventions - Group 2, Adults in Residential Homes

Residents in various care homes received weekly A.R.R.O.W. help through the Bridgwater College Your Skills programs. The residents were experiencing the effects of either Senile Dementia, Stroke and/or Learning Problems. Some 30 residents were initially seen at 2 homes across a three year period.

Residential Homes N = 30   1st Intervention
See appendix 25

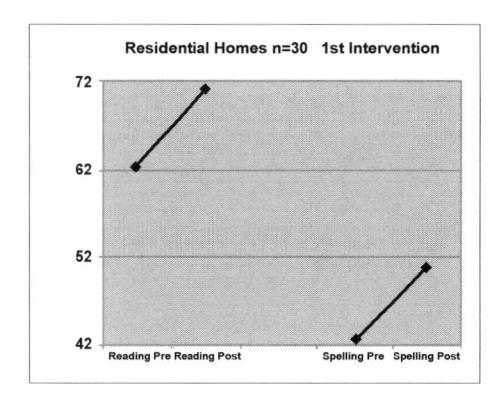

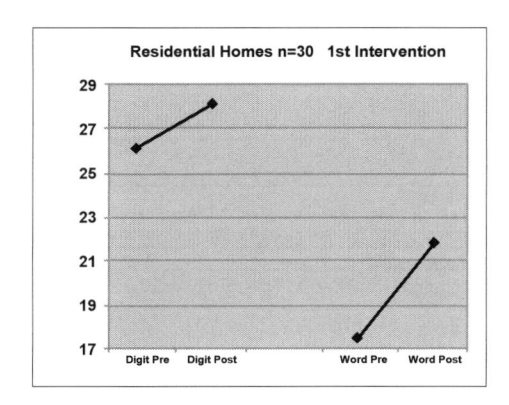

Subjects in the residential homes were often aged 75 years plus, but nevertheless, after one A.R.R.O.W. intervention, made marked improvements in reading skills, spelling skills, and working short term memory for digit and word recall.

- Reading Skills   13.43%   progress after 1st intervention
- Spelling Skills   18.26%   progress after 1st intervention
- Digit Recall   7.18%   progress after 1st intervention
- Word Recall   24.37%   progress after 1st intervention

Evidence shows an improvement in Reading, Spelling and Short Term Memory skills. It was also evident that:

- Immediate and noticeable progress was made once the first intervention had been affected
- There was no regression to the original scores after a 2-3 month delay between the two interventions

A second intervention involving 19 residents from the original 30 showed the trend for improvement continued.

Residential Homes N = 19   2nd Intervention
See appendix 26

- Reading Skills a further   2.5%   progress during 2nd intervention
- Spelling Skills a further   5.18%   progress during 2nd intervention
- Digit Recall   a further   4.8%   progress during 2nd intervention
- Word Recall   a further   4.0%   progress during 2nd intervention

A group of 13 adults were able to undertake three interventions. Reading and spelling results showed a significant increase from the 1st intervention baseline. Digit and Word Recall results show a marked upward movement. The evidence suggests that learning improvements can be effected within the ageing population and suggest that additional A.R.R.O.W. intervention strategies will extend the learning improvements even further. Investigation of the scores show that improvements were on a linear basis with no regression to the original base line levels during the 2-3 months non-intervention periods.

See appendix 27

Results after 3 interventions show the overall improvement against the initial pre-intervention baseline.

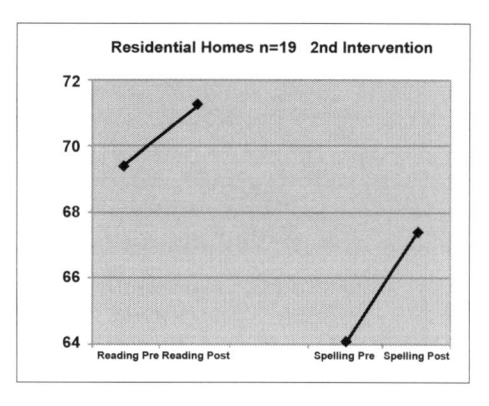

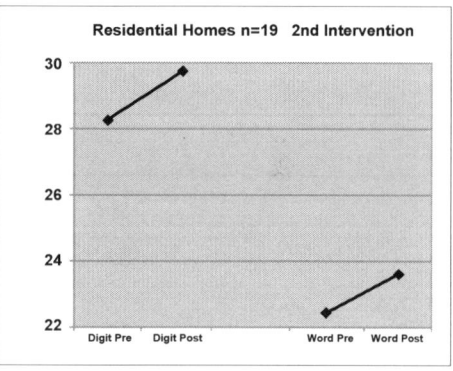

- Reading Skills   21.89%   overall improvement
- Spelling Skills   14.94%   overall improvement
- Digit Recall   5.9%   overall improvement
- Word Recall   30.09%   overall improvement

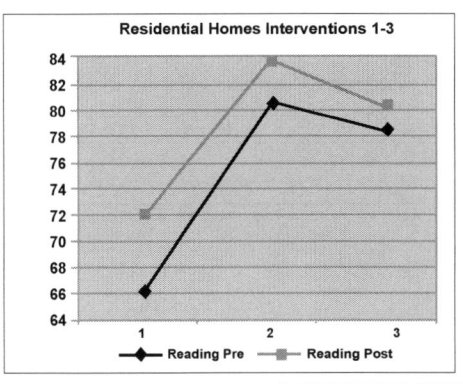

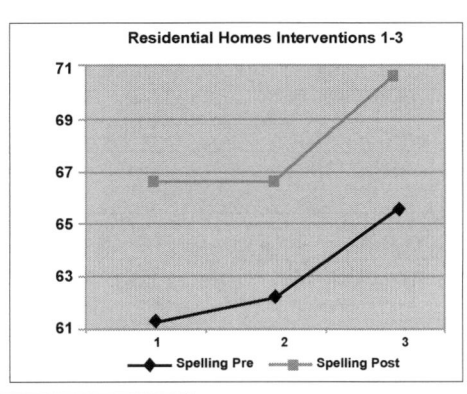

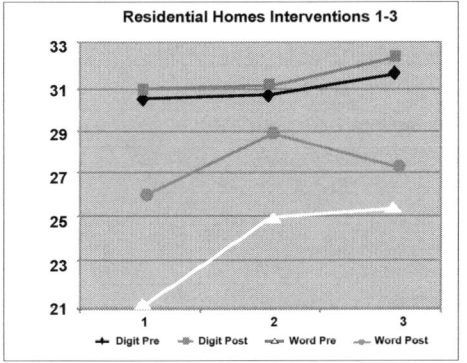

These final results show:

- The non-intervention periods maintain any improved performance when compared to the original intervention commencement scores
- A continuing improvement persists for the adults after three interventions save in the digit recall condition which nevertheless, remains superior to the baseline test score
- An upward progression in learning processes can be obtained with an ageing population

Naomi Mellows, the A.R.R.O.W. tutor with the Residential Home adults states:

"The work with the residential homes was very rewarding for the clients. They made progress and knew it. Some at first thought that the material would be too easy, but once they were confronted with the Self-Voice and demands required of them, realised it was not a school level exercise. They loved the self-teaching aspect of the approach.

Those residents with learning problems acquired a new independence in that they were able to communicate in the outside world and therefore, undertake environmental tasks such as shopping and finding their way around by reading signs. They were able to read labels when before they were trying to remember the colour and shape of the packages. All in all a fantastic exercise."

Group 3, Adults with Severe Learning Problems
General Background
A large number of students were helped who were experiencing severe learning problems through socio-economic and/or processing deficits and also included some with brain injury as a result of traumatic accidents. The Severe Learning Problem groups contained adults with memory loss, language processing and communication difficulties. Evidence is presented from 3 sites where tutors travelled weekly in order to assist the adults. Lessons were of approximately 1 hour duration and the same procedures were followed as for the other adult groups. In 1978, research had shown that school age pupils with Severe Listening and Speech skills, could improve various language skills through A.R.R.O.W. intervention strategies. The question being posed some twenty years later was would the Self-Voice approach similarly help adults with Severe Learning Problems?

Learning Problem Adults
See appendix 28

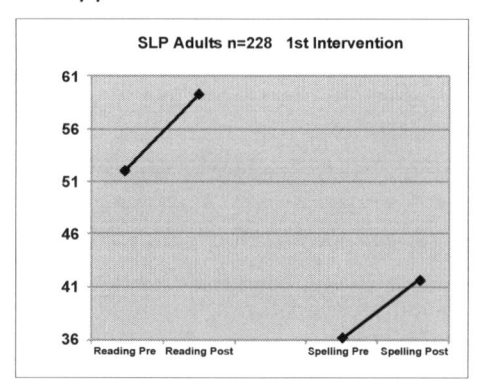

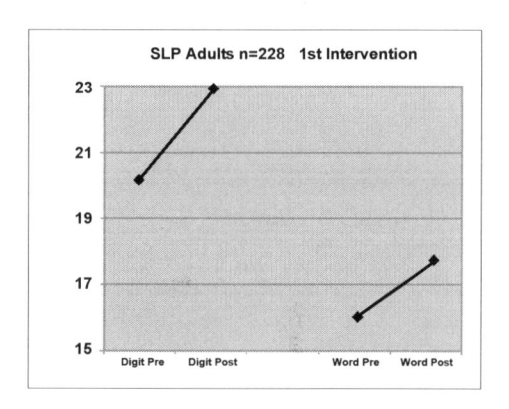

n = 228 1st Intervention
The 3 Severe Learning Problem (SLP) Groups met once weekly and each student received a maximum 1 hour A.R.R.O.W. intervention program during this time.

As with the Stroke and Residential Home Groups, A.R.R.O.W. intervention with SLP students made an immediate and marked improvement in reading skills, spelling skills and working Short Term Memory for Digit and Word Recall.

Pre-Post Test results showed:

- Reading Skills   10.08%   progress during 1st intervention
- Spelling Skills   14.67%   progress during 1st intervention
- Digit Recall   14.14%   progress during 1st intervention
- Word Recall   12.07%   progress during 1st intervention

A group of 166 students formed the second intervention cohort. Further improvements following the first intervention were realised across all tests.

See appendix 29

- Reading Skills a further 8.38% progress during 2nd intervention
- Spelling Skills a further 11.30% progress during 2nd intervention
- Digit Recall a further 8.77% progress during 2nd intervention
- Word Recall a further 16.46% progress during 2nd intervention

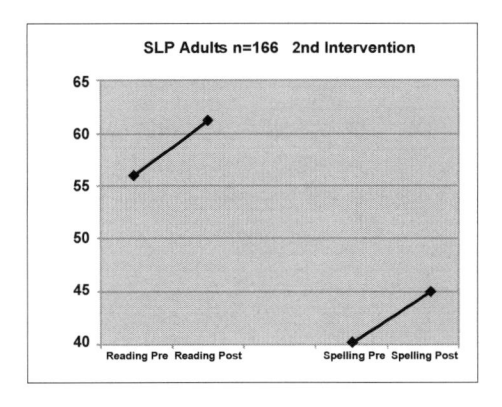

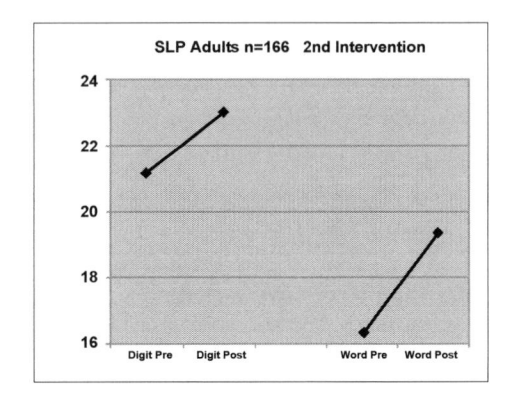

Results show the familiar pattern of improvements made by the CVA and Residential Home groups after the 1st and 2nd interventions.

A group of 12 students were able to undertake 7 interventions. Evidence shows that the starting base line levels for the learning problem group was below that of all other groups, yet improvements in terms of performance still run parallel to the other cohorts. The pattern was again that of accelerated learning when on A.R.R.O.W. intervention and no regression to the original base line during the non-intervention periods.

See appendix 30

- Reading Skills 65.28% overall improvement
- Spelling Skills 35.09% overall improvement
- Digit Recall 15.8% overall improvement
- Word Recall 11.11% overall improvement

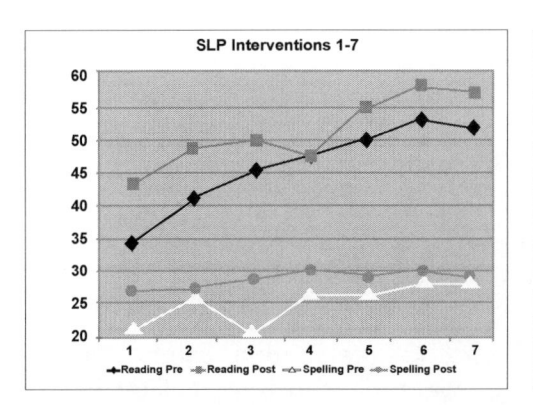

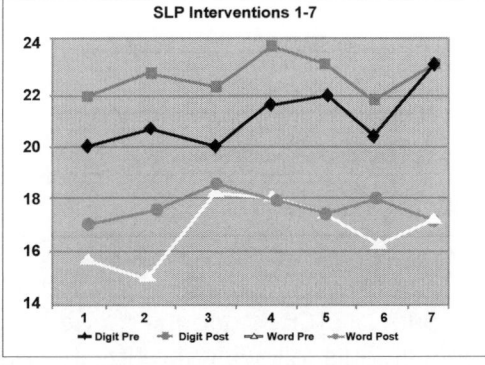

The final results show:
- The non-intervention periods continue to show an improved performance when compared to the original intervention commencement scores
- An overall progression of the students continues after 7 interventions (note regression of word and digit recall after 4 interventions)
- Upward progression in learning processes can be obtained with a population experiencing severe learning problems

A.R.R.O.W. Your Skills Interventions - Group 4, Headway - Adults with Brain Injury
See appendix 31

A discrete group of 13 brain injured adults with problems emanating solely from brain trauma were measured across 4 interventions. Their results follow the pattern of all other groups insofar as there was a marked improvement in Reading, Spelling, Short Term Memory for Digits and Words after the A.R.R.O.W. 'Your Skills' programs. As with the other groups there was no regression to original base line scores.

- Reading Skills   9.66%   progress during 1st intervention
- Spelling Skills   19.55%   progress during 1st intervention
- Digit Recall   14.14%   progress during 1st intervention
- Word Recall   14.08%   progress during 1st intervention

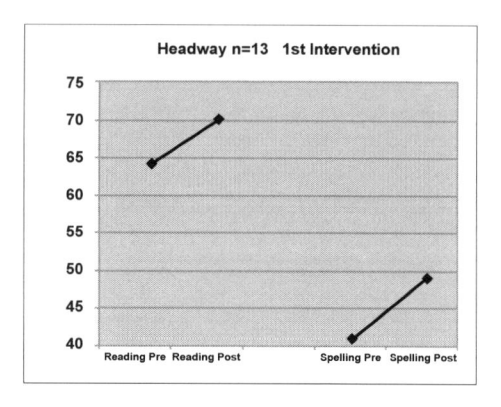

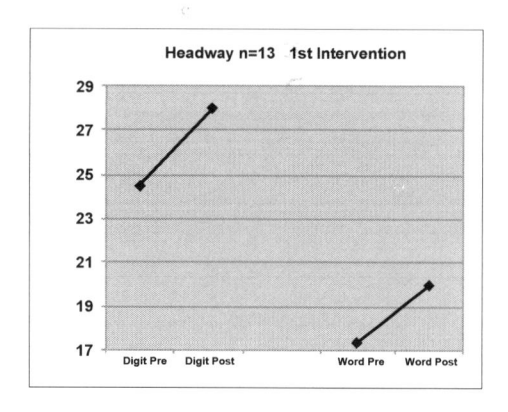

The 2nd intervention results show a familiar upward pattern.
See appendix 32

- Reading Skills a further   8.75%   progress after 2nd intervention
- Spelling Skills a further   14.94%   progress after 2nd intervention
- Digit Recall   a further   8.05%   progress after 2nd intervention
- Word Recall   a further   6.34%   progress after 2nd intervention

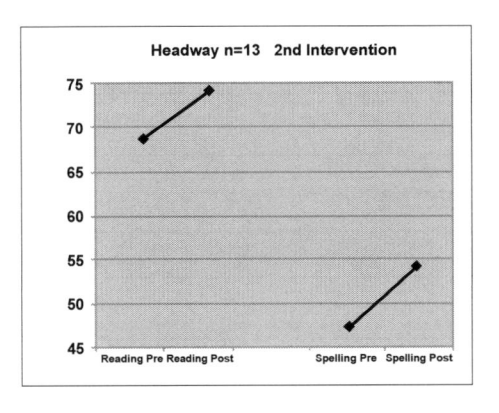

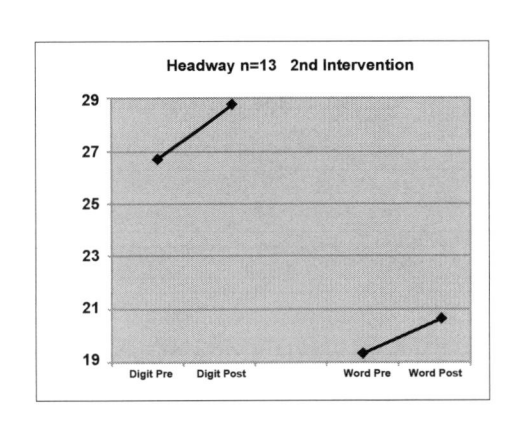

Results from the 4 interventions show a continuous upward learning curve for Reading, Spelling and Short Term Memory for digits and words. As with the CVA, Residential Homes and Severe Learning Problem cohorts, there was no regression to the starting levels of performance during non-intervention periods of 2-3 months duration.

See appendix 33

- Reading Skills   25.76%   overall improvement
- Spelling Skills   50.75%   overall improvement
- Digit Recall   25.75%   overall improvement
- Word Recall   32.13%   overall improvement

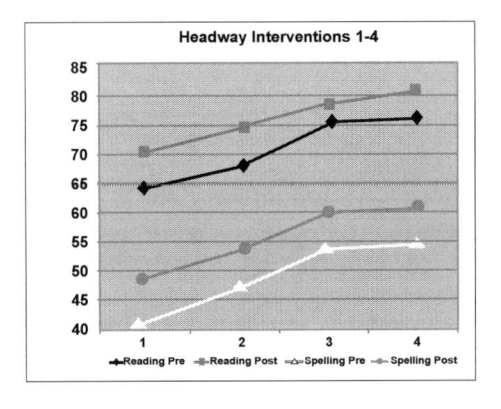

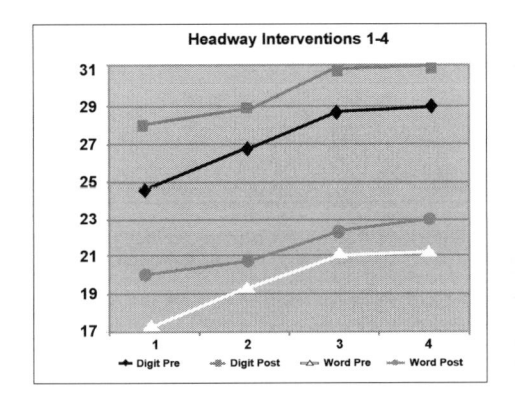

These final results show:

- The non-intervention periods reveal an improved performance when compared to the original intervention commencement scores
- A continuous improvement by the subjects after 4 interventions
- Upward progression in learning processes can be obtained with an adult population suffering from traumatic brain injury

Results discussed
It can be seen that the pattern of improvements gained by the Brain Injury group

of students parallels those obtained by the three other cohorts. On the first intervention, Students with Brain Injury made progress in Reading Skills, Spelling Skills and Short-Term Memory for Digits/Words. This progression continued throughout all 4 interventions and with this group there is no STM fall-off.

DM *"I find that my memory is now quite good. I would like to improve it even more if I can. On the course there's nothing I don't like doing. I enjoy my memory and mostly getting some help. During the time that I've been getting help, I've noticed my recall has begun to improve quite distinctly. I would like help on a more frequent basis."*

MF *"I think the course is wonderful because it makes you come to terms with your head injury. It's given me much more fire in my belly and allowed me to fight."*

LF *"I liked recording my voice. I liked doing computers and my memory and spelling. I was pleased about the course."*

A Social Services Worker from Yeovil writes:
"We are writing to express how much we value the A.R.R.O.W. courses that have been taking place, Simon, the tutor has been excellent, he has been endlessly patient and sensitive to the differing disabilities and needs of our clients. This in turn has made the clients feel very comfortable and aided their learning. Without exception they have all benefited from the course. All have commented on the improvement in either their confidence, speech, memory or concentration. One stroke victim in particular, speech has improved to such an extent that members of her family and friends have commented on the change in her. They have all expressed a wish to continue…we cannot emphasize enough how highly we rate the A.R.R.O.W. courses, we have seen first hand the benefits our clients have gained from this innovative approach to learning".

Another Social Worker Writes:
"All clients have shown a clear improvement in the areas that your course covers, such as reading, writing, listening, memory, spelling and problem solving. I am also pleased to include an increase in confidence with some as well."

Unit Manager of a local branch of Headway writes:
"On behalf of Headway…working so successfully with some of our clients…The results that I witnessed within the centre were most impressive…we shall be very pleased for you to return…"

Chapter 8 Conclusion
A.R.R.O.W. is helping adults in the community who have learning and/or communication problems. A 'Your Skills' course was introduced under the auspices of A.R.R.O.W. and Bridgwater College and appropriate tutors trained. Exploratory visits were made which established the viability of future Community Group work involving Adults with Stroke, Adults in Residential Care, those at

Learning Centres or Centres for Adults with Brain Injury. Early work with an adult with Stroke and at a Liverpool Centre for Dysphasic Adults, showed that A.R.R.O.W. could benefit adults' reading, spelling, working short term memory and speech. Work with an adult suffering from Altzheimer's was extremely encouraging and showed that comprehension skills were more effective when listening to the Self-Voice than to any other. A lady with meningitis and very poor literacy and communication skills gained much benefit from a systematic approach to word recall and recognition using A.R.R.O.W. A young man with a traumatic brain injury greatly improved his speech skills after A.R.R.O.W. whilst an adult with Autism made considerable progress in his comprehension and word recognition skills after the Self-Voice approach. Common core problems for adults with literacy and communication problems are identified as Speech, Listening, Reading, Writing, Working Short Term Memory, Behavioural Shifts, Relationships with Others, and Loss of Co-ordination. A.R.R.O.W. Tutors were specially selected for the 'Your Skills' course and delivered interventions on a weekly basis, 1 hour per week across 10 weeks. The course included work on Comprehension, Free Writing, Survival Words and Spellings. Learning material is differentiated for the 4 identifiable groups of adults whilst Reading and Spelling Tests used a % improvement baseline measurement. Group 1, Adults with CVA (Stroke), made substantial improvements in literacy and memory based tasks and maintained these across 6 interventions. A case study of an adult with Stroke shows that communication skills greatly improved after Split Record and Echoing techniques were employed when working at a weekly club or at home. The Self-Voice techniques, including those involving singing and memory training based upon life experiences are described. Observations from the wife of the adult with Stroke, two Stroke Club Managers' and a Speech and Language Therapist are noted, together with comments from adults. Group 2, Adults in Residential Homes, made marked and sustained progress in literacy and memory skills across 3 interventions. The A.R.R.O.W. Tutor made positive comments about the new found independence of the adults after Self-Voice. Group 3, Adults with Learning Problems, was initially a large population of some 228 adults. Improvements were gained against the literacy and memory batch of tests and the literacy test results continued to improve for those 12 students able to undertake 7 interventions. Memory Skills however, appeared to peak on the final 2 interventions. Group 4, Adults with Brain Injury, made considerable and sustained progress across the literacy and memory assessments. Student and Social Worker comments were most positive and attested to the success of the interventions.

Chapter 9
A.R.R.O.W. in Specialised Sites

Job Seeker Adults with Literacy Difficulties 122

A Customised A.R.R.O.W. Driving Test Program 122

Word Attack Skills 123

Spelling Skills 123

Basic Skills Assessment 123

Time on A.R.R.O.W. 123

Higher Ability Job Seekers 123

Less Able and More Able Job Seekers 124

Consultant Observations 124
      Case Studies 124

Assessment of Word Attack Skills after 4-5 Hours A.R.R.O.W. 125

Movement within the Basic Skills Version 2 Assessment 126

Self-Esteem Comments 126

Specialist Residential Care Centre - Literacy and Communication
Improvements 127

Staff Tutor Training 128

A Residential Home specialising in Autism 129

A.R.R.O.W. Rapid Learning Two Hour Exeter Project 129

Student Selection 129

Results 130

Adults Self-Assessment of Progress 131

Chapter 9 Conclusion 131

Chapter 9
A.R.R.O.W. in Specialised Sites

There are many occasions when A.R.R.O.W. has been used most successfully outside the mainstream educational remit. Three examples are given which show the far reaching applications of the approach for adults with various learning needs. The first example of A.R.R.O.W. relates to its use with Job Seeker adults experiencing literacy difficulties. The second example relates to its use within a Specialist Care Centre whilst the third example shows its use as a most rapid learning strategy for literacy improvement. Reactions of a tutor helping adults with severe autism are noted.

Job Seeker Adults with Literacy Difficulties
Ten Job Seekers attended Basic Skills courses in a South Wales Training Centre. The Training Provider requested help from A.R.R.O.W. in order to raise literacy standards. The Job Seeker population at the Training Centre varied in literacy skill ability, but the overall picture was one of a great need to further improve literacy and/or communication skills in order to obtain employment within the workplace. Part of the Job Seekers training was the use of Computerised Driving Simulators. The Simulators were used to help the Job Seekers pass their Driving Test and it was decided to design customised A.R.R.O.W. material for this purpose, in addition to raising generic literacy skills.

A Customised A.R.R.O.W. Driving Test Program
The job seekers followed a customised A.R.R.O.W. 5-8 hour program for one week based upon components of the Driving Test. The A.R.R.O.W. Driving Test Topic material was ability graded and followed the overall 'tried and trusted' pattern established within the mainstream education sector. The Driving Test program had the added bonus of being central to the adult's specific needs at that time. Students saw movie sequences involving five driving scenarios used for Topic passages:

1. Motorway Rules
2. Lanes and Hard Shoulders
3. The Speed Limit
4. Hazard Awareness
5. Roundabouts

After referring to a movie sequence, each student undertook an appropriate topic. Each topic was followed by spellings taken from the customized passages. The spellings followed the standard A.R.R.O.W. format in which the printed word was first shown on screen, then spoken aloud before being presented as a series of letters forming the words. The student therefore recorded the word and associated letters before playing these back when undertaking Self-Voice dictation.

Word Attack Skills
Word attack scores for the 10 adults averaged 48 words correctly recognised - realising an average reading age of 9 years 5 months. The lowest attainer scored 12 correct - a reading age of 6 years 10 months. The most able scored 100 words correct - a ceiling for the test and some 6 years ahead of the least able adult.

Spelling Skills
Spellings for the adults averaged 31.33 words correctly spelt – realising an average spelling age of 8 years 2 months. The lowest attainer scored 4 correct – a spelling age of 5 years 5 months. The most able scored 72 correct – a spelling age of 12 years 3 months, ie, almost 7 years in advance of the lowest achieving adult.

The seven year literacy range of the students would obviously test the flexibility of A.R.R.O.W. to deal with students who were either in their late teens, or early-mid twenties and included some of whom were disaffected by previous school based experiences.

Basic Skills Assessment
The average score for the 10 Job Seekers on the Basic Skills Version 2 Literacy Assessment Introductory Level was 45.3. This presents an average for the cohort of 2.2 - the lower end of the Entry 2 Level. The lowest attainer scored 15 correct i.e. within the Entry Level 1 standard whilst the highest attainer scored 61 correct, i.e. the upper range of the Entry 3.

Further investigation revealed the association between the A.R.R.O.W. Reading and Spelling tests and those of Basic Skills. A correlation of 0.72p was realised between the A.R.R.O.W. Word Reading test and Basic Skill assessment and suggests that a single word reading test is a good predictor of success in the Basic Skills Assessment. A correlation of 0.86p was realised between the spelling test adopted by A.R.R.O.W. and Basic Skills assessment – this is a high correlation and also proves the worth of the single word spelling measure as a predictor of success in the Basic Skills Assessment.

Time on A.R.R.O.W.
The usual time allocated for adult students on A.R.R.O.W. is between 6 and 10 hours work for an intervention involving some 6-10 programs. The Job Seekers had slightly less time than this i.e. 6-8 hours and all testing was conducted inside this time schedule. This meant that "training" time was actually less than 5 hours for the students. The customised programs used in the project, consisted of one topic per session based upon the Driving Theory Test and spellings based upon words presented in the topic.

Higher Ability Job Seekers
It became apparent that the more able Job Seekers could readily complete their A.R.R.O.W. allocation of work within 5-6 hours and would have required

additional material in order to follow a full 10 hour program.

Less Able and More Able Job Seekers
It was felt that there were several Job Seekers achieving low scores who could make rapid and sustained progress given the opportunity. It was also apparent that some less able Job Seekers would require a full 10 hours in order to indicate their true potential. The Personal Spelling Profile feature of A.R.R.O.W., in which a learner improves spelling skills by practising specific word families not currently known to them, would prove of great benefit to the lower achieving Job Seekers. The higher ability students would clearly benefit from undertaking specific spellings taken from their Driving Test Passage.

Consultant Observations
By the second A.R.R.O.W. 1 hour session, consultants in the Training Centre had noticed that the Job Seekers had already began to make progress in reading and spelling skills, handwriting and general presentation, whilst also showing greater confidence and self-esteem than previously.

Case Studies
1. A Job Seeker from Gambia had higher-than-normal literacy skills for the cohort. The benefits of using the A.R.R.O.W. Self-Voice approach for this student, gave him additional experiences in English speech and language work, particularly in monitoring and evaluating his production of speech patterns. He commented that he had never before realised some of his articulation skills were in need of improvement, as his tutors in the Gambia who helped him in English work, were themselves not producing certain English speech sounds in an appropriate manner.

2. A Job Seeker undertook the programs who had been taught in a Welsh-speaking school. His English and word reading skills were the highest of the group. His spelling skills however, fell far below his reading standard and this he found unacceptable. This student undertook a five-hour program in order to improve his spelling progress.

3. A Job Seeker student scored very low on the spelling test. He showed pleasant surprise on hearing his own voice replayed and following the first session, began to improve his literacy and overall confidence. Handwriting was an issue for him and was also addressed using A.R.R.O.W.

4. A Hearing Impaired student, silently mouthed the recorded material as it was played back to him, thereby giving evidence of internal speech - talking to oneself in one's head. A.R.R.O.W. had the added benefit of improving the student's literacy performances and also his speech and auditory attention - skills so essential in the workplace.

The evidence from the Job Seekers' positive attitude towards the Self-Voice work, together with clinical observation by tutors and managers, indicated that

A.R.R.O.W. could be a major factor towards helping move Job Seekers into the work place.

The rapidity of progress in skill learning was a most important feature of A.R.R.O.W. and was particularly appropriate for Job Seekers who had not realised their potential within the school-based educational system. The use of customised, vocation-directed material proved of particular benefit. A.R.R.O.W. is extremely flexible in its application so that under a different timetabling structure, the project could have been administered within two weeks, an hour a day, for ten days, with the less able students. Higher ability Job Seekers could however, have easily completed their tasks within five hours. ie one week.

Assessment of Word Attack Skills after 4-5 Hours A.R.R.O.W.

After 4-5 hours A.R.R.O.W. all attendees of the Job Seekers team were given the post A.R.R.O.W. word attack reading test. Before and after results are impressive.

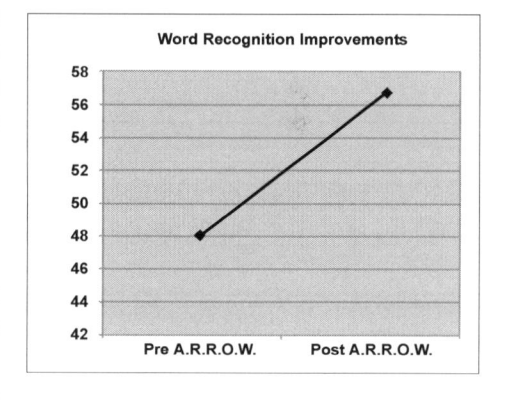

See appendix 34

The group reading gains were equivalent to 8 months progress in word attack skills after less than 5 hours A.R.R.O.W. Driving Theory Training. It was noticeable that the students were approaching the literacy improvement task with considerable enthusiasm. There were no absentees during the five lesson project. It became apparent that work place material, rather than mainstream school curriculum programmes used in most interventions, had been instrumental in raising a student's word recognition skills.

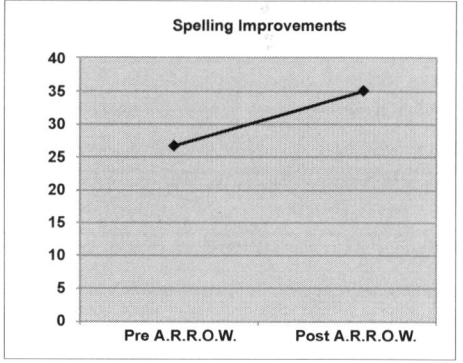

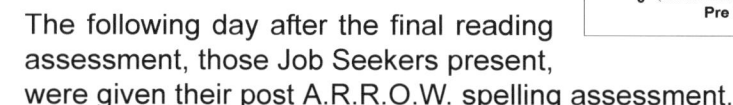

The following day after the final reading assessment, those Job Seekers present, were given their post A.R.R.O.W. spelling assessment.

See Appendix 35

There was most marked improvements in spelling performances - the average improvement for the cohort being 10+ months spelling progress in 5 hours A.R.R.O.W. These results are thought to be amongst the finest achieved by any group teaching system, given the short time span allowed.

Movement within the Basic Skills Version 2 Assessment

All Job Seekers, for whom data was available, made positive improvements on Basic Skills Version 2. One Job Seeker moved from Entry Level 2 to Level 1, two others moved even further from Entry Level 3 to Level 1. The implications of these shifts are, of course, considerable for the future progress of the Job Seekers, but also reveal the cost effectiveness of A.R.R.O.W. when dramatically and rapidly improving students' literacy levels.

Self-Esteem Comments

The Job Seekers were asked to rank their reading and spelling skills before and after they undertook the A.R.R.O.W. 4-5 hour program. Ranking was on a five point scale without reference to any discrete components of A.R.R.O.W. as later developed for the mainstream education self-assessment.

5 Very Good	4 Good	3 Neither good Nor bad	2 Bad	1 Very Bad
Reading self-appraisal before A.R.R.O.W. Reading self-appraisal after A.R.R.O.W.		Averaged 2.5 Averaged 3.6 = **44%** increase in self worth.		
Spelling self-appraisal before A.R.R.O.W. Spelling self-appraisal after A.R.R.O.W.		Averaged 2.3 Averaged 3.5 = **52%** increase in self worth.		
These positive self rankings by students are borne out by comments made by the same students when later interviewed about their performances.				

The Job Seekers were asked questions about the project:

Has A.R.R.O.W. helped you?
Do you feel better about yourself?
Is A.R.R.O.W. different from how you've learned before?
Other comments.

Answers given include:

L "It's helped me an awful lot with my spelling and writing as well…
   I feel better about myself reading and writing.
   At school they would learn you but then you'd completely forget about it.
   I could go on doing it and get better still."

R "I can spell better – before I couldn't spell at all, now I can a bit.
   I feel good, I feel better outside with my mates.
   I like doing this, tidy, it's fun really cause you hear yourself talking back.
   I want it to go on."

C "It's helped me concentrate.
I'm happier with myself because I'm reading and writing a bit better.
This is a better way of learning – a chance of getting a job at the end of it."

S "It's helped my spelling – working the computer I've noticed it's helped my reading some words I didn't know before.
I feel a little bit more confident.
I've never done much voice work on the computer before. I found it a bit hard to talk louder."

Cal "It has helped me by showing me what to do – it has helped my listening. Never done this before, sometimes my voice helps me – I like good speech."

J "I can pronounce words better. I don't feel any different about myself.
A lot different from school – I didn't do anything with my own voice at school – I don't mind my own voice."

Results are very exciting for word reading and spelling skills of Job Seekers after 6-8 hours A.R.R.O.W. The students' own positive self-assessments of their progress fully confirm their rise in self-worth after A.R.R.O.W. An added bonus was that the marked and lasting literacy improvement which used 'real world', i.e. Driving Theory Test material. The use of existing Training Centre staff for over viewing and administrative tasks proved to be a most successful and attractive feature of the pilot and led to two members being trained to deliver A.R.R.O.W. within their centre.

Specialist Residential Care Centre - Literacy and Communication Improvements

Described by BBC 'Tomorrow's World' (1996) as, 'A.R.R.O.W.'s most significant success', the work conducted at Ty Gwyn Hall Independent Hospital, a Specialist Residential Care Centre in South Wales, has proved a source of inspiration for many tutors. The Centre was established for students with Severe Psychiatric and Personality disorders experiencing severe speech/language problems together with associated literacy skill deficits. After an initial series of visits by the author, staff at the centre were trained as tutors, obtained the necessary audio recorders and books and worked with the residents. The adults then began to utilise the DVD computer system once this was introduced. The residents followed the standard A.R.R.O.W. format in which a tutor first assessed the reading and spelling levels, before placing a student on appropriate A.R.R.O.W. programs. The tutor assisted the student to record the necessary spelling and topic material before leaving the student to operate the system with minimal supervision. Training time was dependent upon the student's wishes, but was usually 2-3 times per week with lessons of 30 minutes maximum duration.

Staff Tutor Training
After the success of the initial work by the author, selected staff were given A.R.R.O.W. Tutor Training and began to both assess the students and implement the programs.

After several months the Manager, when interviewed, spoke of the impact of A.R.R.O.W.
"The thing I noticed was the enthusiasm the residents showed for it especially when they had learnt how to use it themselves…"

The progress of one student was featured in the TV programme. Sue was a resident of some 40+ years who first attended the centre for three years prior to meeting A.R.R.O.W. She had literacy problems and could neither relate to, trust, or communicate with other people due to her aggressive non-cooperative moods. When she began A.R.R.O.W. Sue changed dramatically. Her ability to read and write vastly improved and with it her confidence.

The Manager continues:
"…this lady had no self-esteem. You could not sit down and talk to her at all. Now she is able to express herself so much better, it's unbelievable. I'm sure anyone who nursed Sue before would find it hard to believe she's so focused."

Sue:
"I don't mind doing this because it helps me and when I go into society again I'll know how to cope and that. Everybody can do it if they try, if they get the right teacher they can do it. It really is marvellous."

The TV programme presenter summarises:
"No one's sure why A.R.R.O.W. had the impact it had but for many, her case is recommendation enough. At the age of 45 she's taken a job at the local hospital, her first step back into the outside world."

Another Care Home Manager at the same site wrote several years later:
"A.R.R.O.W. has been facilitated within this unit for over 5 years, and during this time a number of significant improvements have been noted from clients who engage with this project. We as a team, have noted many improvements in several of our clients as they have progressed with A.R.R.O.W.

1. *Improvements in their fluency of reading, including comprehension, tone and volume of speech.*
2. *Improvements in syntax and spelling.*
3. *Improvements in legibility of handwriting, which is now consistently well formed with some residents' cursive.*

4. Improvements in concentration and attention span.

Many of the residents engaged upon the A.R.R.O.W. programs have missed out on educational opportunities in the past. They are now receiving input through your programs and often verbalise the positive effects it is having on their confidence and skills."

A visitor to the Centre wrote:
"A.R.R.O.W. engages the interest of the clients who appear to be otherwise almost beyond the reach of education; adults with virtually no literacy skills. It finds within these people the will to improve their sociability, literacy and verbal expression. The system offers them an image of themselves as dignified individuals, better engaged and more intelligent than they had believed themselves to be. That is perhaps why it works so powerfully as a motivating tool for self improvement...who can estimate the value of giving back a chunk of humanity to a long-term institutionalised mental patient. It seems to me that the system used by Bridgwater College is one of such extraordinary and subtle power..." (Lord Craigmyle 2006).

A Residential Home specialising in Autism

A residential home for Adults with Autism in the South West of England has recently had members of staff trained in A.R.R.O.W. and introduced the system to their service users. The response from the first cohort of four adults and tutors has been most encouraging. One tutor comments:

"I think it is a fantastic program. The clarity of the service users' speech when using A.R.R.O.W. is most marked and so much better than it has been previously. Each person I have worked with has a much better attention span than previously and it has generalised to other projects. To me, they genuinely enjoy A.R.R.O.W. and it has improved their reading, writing and memory. Other members of staff have commented on the difference and improvements. Tom has even asked for homework." Elizabeth Kelly

A.R.R.O.W. Rapid Learning Two Hour Exeter Project

An unusual intervention project was completed with 11 adult volunteers during 2008. It was decided to investigate whether an A.R.R.O.W. reading and spelling literacy intervention could be effective for adults when taken within a single 2-3 hour morning or afternoon session. It was also decided to find out the opinions of the adults towards establishing an A.R.R.O.W. adult drop-in facility within the work place.

Student Selection

Students within the Exeter intervention were volunteers who were given a pre-course assessment for reading and spelling during the 3 hour intervention which therefore, resulted in a 'true' working time of 2 hours per student.

Two of the students were found to be above average in terms of reading and spelling. Nine other students however, experienced literacy problems. All 11 volunteer students attended the morning or afternoon session. The average reading score for the students was 58.81 marks out of a possible 100 realising an average reading age of 10 years 2 months. The average spelling score was 41.36 out of a possible 100 realising an average spelling age of 9 years 2 months. The students were assessed individually for word reading, and within a group, for spelling.

Students attended in two groups, in the morning (n=5) or afternoon (n=6). They worked for 3 hours maximum including a 20 minute rest interval. The Students undertook the recording, replay, writing and self marking tasks independently for the duration of the programs. Despite being in close proximity with each other, the students maintained maximum concentration during the 3 hour programs.

After the tests were administered, the students were allocated appropriate A.R.R.O.W. reading/spelling programs. In order to establish non-bias during assessments, the A.R.R.O.W. tutor was observed testing students by the Work Place Centre Manager and the Manager of a Training Agency.

Each program was based on the student's own personal requirements in terms of reading ability and spelling. The more advanced students worked on topics and spellings designed for military personnel. The less able students worked on topics and spellings used in colleges and schools. No student reported that they felt patronised by the content of the material.

The students undertook two main Self-Voice tasks; the learning of spellings through word families and/or words taken from Advanced Topics together with improvement of reading skills through ability related topics. Results were extremely encouraging:
See appendix 36

Results
An average of six months progress was realised in word recognition within 2 hours concentrated work. Spelling improvements showed an average 4 months improvement within 2 hours. Both sets of improvements would appear to be ground breaking insofar as:

- The results are equivalent to those obtained within several A.R.R.O.W. sessions
- No adults had previously met A.R.R.O.W. in this manner

The results are equivalent to, if not superior to those sometimes obtained within the mainstream education sector. It is most encouraging that the adults, many of whom had experienced failure in previous attempts to improve their reading and spelling skills, were able to raise their standards within a very short period of time.

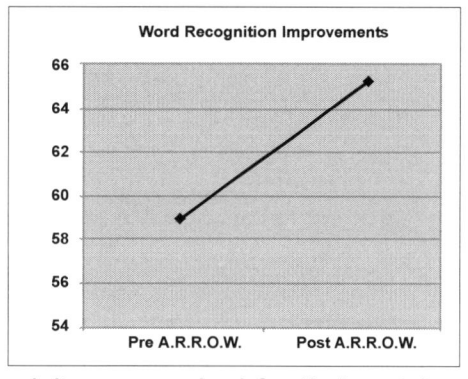

Word Recognition Improvements (chart showing increase from ~59 Pre A.R.R.O.W. to ~65 Post A.R.R.O.W.)

Adults Self-Assessment of Progress
During a post-intervention discussion, the adults were asked for their opinions as to the appeal and effectiveness of A.R.R.O.W. Their views may be summarised thus:

- The approach had certainly helped reading and spelling
- The adults generally felt they would be prepared to undertake the programs on a drop-in basis
- The participating adults also felt others would benefit
- The use of the A.R.R.O.W. Self-Voice was an important part of the process

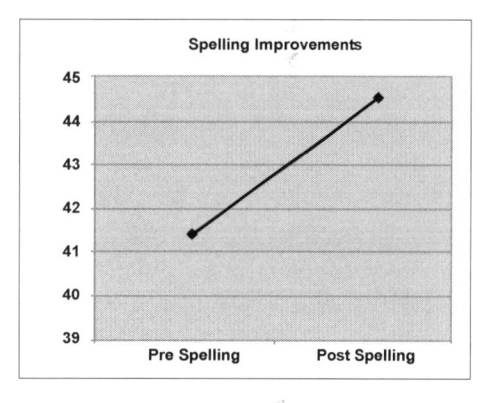

Spelling Improvements (chart showing increase from ~41 Pre Spelling to ~44.5 Post Spelling)

It was obvious that if the adults had been able to receive further A.R.R.O.W., then even higher level of literacy standards could have been expected. The improved results arose from a scheme which resulted in minimum work place disruption compared to an adult attending a somewhat lengthy college course or accessing a private tutor, itself a costly exercise for the student. Once an initial outlay had been made and an A.R.R.O.W. tutor had been trained, the system would operate in a highly cost effective manner. The circumstances surrounding the innovative trial meant that A.R.R.O.W. was put under intense scrutiny in terms of implementation. The system however, operated beyond expectations. Given the opportunity to establish a work place centre which followed a more relaxed and efficient set of testing procedures, it would be reasonable to expect even stronger results.

Chapter 9 Conclusion
Three discrete interventions with adults outside the mainstream educational remit and experiencing literacy problems, were undertaken in Wales and South West England. These adults are identified as Job Seekers, Adults with Personality Disorders and Students in the Workplace. Ten Job Seekers were receiving help from a Training Provider who utilised Driving Simulators as part of an overall program. The Provider requested support and a customized Driving Test A.R.R.O.W. program was developed. Average Reading Age scores

for the Job Seekers was 9 years 5 months constituting a 7 year ability range between lowest and highest achievers. Spelling Skills averaged a 7.7 year level, with a 7 year ability span between students. Basic Skills Assessments were made and showed a close association between the A.R.R.O.W. Literacy Tests and Basic Skills measures of progress. Time on A.R.R.O.W. was less than 5 hours, with the higher ability students completing their programs faster than the less proficient. Student reactions and Training Provider Consultant observations were most encouraging. Case Studies showed that Speech, English as an Additional Language, Voice Acceptance and Sub-Vocalisation processes were positively influenced by A.R.R.O.W. Word attack and spelling skills progressed after the short intervention. Basic Skills performances also improved during the one week period. Literacy and Communication improvements were observed during work at a Residential Care Centre for Adults with Personality Disorders. The success of A.R.R.O.W. was such that Care Staff were so encouraged they began to deliver A.R.R.O.W. themselves on a daily basis to the residents, several of whom could work independently of the tutor once a recording was made. A single Case Study demonstrated the effectiveness of the approach and the life style change it effected with one particular resident. Managers and Visitors to the Centre endorsed the use of the approach. A Tutor at a residential centre for Adults with Autism commented most favourably upon the use of the system. A.R.R.O.W. was used in a Rapid Learning Format in Devon, involving eleven adults who undertook two 1 hour sessions delivered within a morning or afternoon. The adult volunteers undertook the shortened program as a result of their perceived literacy problems. An average improvement of 6 months reading progress was recorded by the adults together with 4 months spelling within the one day program. The adult's self-assessed their progress and felt it had certainly helped reading/spelling skills and welcomed the idea of its application on a drop in basis to also include others with literacy problems. The Self-Voice approach was placed under considerable surveillance during the one day intervention program but nevertheless, proved its worth. The interventions showed the great impact of A.R.R.O.W. Reading and spelling skills improved across all three cohorts and many of the adult learner students, expressed a very positive attitude to the Self-Voice approach. Some adults had a rise in self-esteem and confidence and proved yet again that A.R.R.O.W. is multifaceted in both its application and the most positive effects achieved with widely differing populations.

Chapter 10
Listening Skill Improvements

Listening – A Lost Art 134

Listening Differences 135

Learning to Listen 135

Relationship between Listening Deficit and Literacy Skills 136

Lane - Listening and Literacy Experiments 136

Bellamy - Listening Experiments 136

Recent Independent Studies 137

The Improvement of Listening Skills with School Age Students 137

The Teaching Methods during the Pre-A.R.R.O.W. Control Period 138

A.R.R.O.W. Intervention Period Results 138

The Classroom Listening Test 139

Suffolk Project – An Independent Study 139

Listening Improvements with Hearing Impaired Adults 140

Listening Improvements and Career Progress 141

The Bridlington Experiment 142

Listening Improvements with Normally Hearing Adults 142

Listening Improvements – Adults with Communication Problems 143

Discussion 144

Non verbal training to improve speech perception in noise 144

Chapter 10 Conclusion 145

Chapter 10
Listening Skill Improvements

Listening – A Lost Art
Educators frequently stress the lack of listening skills amongst the school age population. There are many reasons to account for this sad situation. One reason is undoubtedly the lessening of listening experiences for children if compared to those encountered by previous generations. As a child, the author and his brother were sometimes taken on cycle rides by their parents. They would soon leave home and cycle out into leafy Warwickshire towards Weatheroak Hill. Just before 'Weatheroak' they would turn right, cycle on a little, and then rest their bikes against a five-bar gate. The author's father would point out the direction of several counties including, Warwickshire, Worcestershire, and Herefordshire. When leaning on the fence they would often just look and listen to birdsong and cows in the field. At home each evening, the radio was a point of focus and the author and his brother would listen to a nightly serial, 'Dick Barton Special Agent', before going to bed. Conversation over the meal table was paramount. Part of the mealtime conversation involved turn taking before speaking. All of these exercises, of course, enhanced the vital skill of listening – auditory attention.

The environment was undoubtedly much quieter during the 1940's - 1950's and indeed for several years afterwards. Few homes had television and the introduction of background music in shops and pubs was in its early infancy. Traffic and the resultant increase in surrounding noise were not of the same density or volume as that experienced today.

At the author's Junior School, the listening experience continued to prevail. The author's Year 6 Class Teacher, Mr Gent, would let the class rest their heads on their hands, close their eyes and listen to a story he read when he was seated at his desk, or when moving around the classroom. Once a week, as a reward for good work, the class would listen to programs linked from a radio in the Head's study to speakers in the corner of each classroom, yet again emphasising the auditory experience.

As a practising teacher in his early career, the author well remembers that the listening skill was still all important to the school day. Classes of 40 children would sit in rows and attend to their teacher. Working noise levels within a classroom were usually so quiet that the sound of a pencil dropping on the floor was easily detectable. Some of today's pupils, for whatever reason, have hardly ever experienced such moments of quiet or had enough positive pre-school listening experiences and are negatively affected because of this. Over the last few decades some schools began to tolerate a higher level of classroom noise than previously. In 1987 the author visited an East Midlands open-plan school where adjoining class areas were divided by 1-2 metre high wooden partitions.

Noise levels at the school were unacceptable and peaked at 88 dB on a sound level meter – a point at which both teaching staff and pupils should have worn ear protectors. In 2008, a Lancashire school reported to the author that boys from a socially deprived family spoke in American accents copied from TV cartoons due to a complete lack of conversation/listening experiences when at home.

Listening Differences

We all listen differently. Some people are good listeners, others are not. It is important to clearly establish that differences exist between listening – a pattern of behaviour, and hearing - a faculty. The listening skill is not entirely dependent upon an intact hearing system, but is observed as an ability, which varies from child to child or adult to adult amongst the normally hearing, or Hearing Impaired populations.

A survey undertaken by the author showed that teachers, when undertaking a background noise listening test, will vary greatly in their ability to identify the spoken word even when placed equidistant from the sound source. A group of 7 Irish tutors were tested and achieved scores of 63, 44, 51, 32, 38, 48, 47, from a 100, i.e. there was a 43% difference between two teachers sitting side by side, (63-44) and 96% difference between the highest and lowest achievers, (63-32). This difference in listening is consistently observed when testing children and adults. Recent U.S.A. research reported in Biology (2017) confirms this earlier A.R.R.O.W. work insofar as hearing impaired adults differed in their speech detection ability when background noise was introduced.

Learning to Listen

Aircrews in World War II, reported that electronic communication through basic headsets was initially very poor, but seemingly improved after a period of several weeks. The aircrews when undergoing training had in fact learned how to listen more attentively. When a student, the author once undertook a summer job working in a bottling factory and found the ambient noise levels almost unbearable in terms of communicating with other workers. After a short while, the author learnt to listen through this noise and, utilising face reading, was able to communicate with colleagues. Other part time or full time factory workers have since confirmed this learning effect.

Ship-to-shore Morse Code operators in South West England, commented to the author that it was not the learning and application of the Morse Code system itself which was the sole cause of their problems when trying to acquire a satisfactory level of proficiency. Much of the operators' early difficulties were caused by atmospheric and acoustic disturbance around the Morse signal (Walton 1982). After a period of some 6 weeks they reported that they had learnt to listen and detect the target Morse Code signal by ignoring the background acoustic disturbances. Hearing Impaired children at a Middle School in Somerset had received regular A.R.R.O.W. speech/language training. Tests conducted in 1985-6, showed they were more effective at identifying their own voices for sentences, lists of words or even a single vowel than Normally Hearing children of the same age. It is suggested, that this surprising finding in favour of the Hearing Impaired students, was a direct result of them learning to listen more effectively to the Self-Voice than their non-Hearing Impaired mainstream peers. It is likely that their superior own-voice identification skills, were due to the amount of Self-Voice listening they had experienced when using A.R.R.O.W. communication training.

Relationship between Listening Deficit and Literacy Skills

In general, it is accepted that the importance of listening is critical to the acquisition of language and literacy skills. Sally Goddard in her work, 'A Teacher's Window Into the Child's Mind' makes the point that various techniques exist for the improvement of listening tasks (Goddard 1996). Maria Chivers (2004) writes that, in Britain, it is accepted that many children with learning difficulties have hearing problems, which in some cases may be temporary but can nevertheless lead to literacy problems. She also observes that listening can be improved by Self-Voice work.

In an unpublished study in Somerset, conducted during the years 1980-90, Cole (1995) reported that 87%+ of students with a 4 year reading deficit showed scar tissue on their ear drums due to a variety of causes including earlier ear infections. In a major study completed in 1979, Conrad (ibid) found that 16+ year old deaf school leavers had a marked reading/spelling deficit and in fact, were operating at a 9 year old literacy level despite having the normal range of intelligence. It is sad to report that despite strenuous efforts since the Conrad findings, it appears that little progress has been realised in improving hearing impaired students' academic performance compared to their normally hearing peers.

Lane - Listening and Literacy Experiments

The author investigated the relationship between listening in noise and literacy skills amongst pupils with normal hearing. An opportunity sample of 113 nine year old children from a Middle School in Somerset, were given a Classroom Listening Test. The students were required to write down twenty short sentences or phrases, presented on tape. All of the children were capable of satisfactorily completing the test to a 95% accuracy level when attending to a quiet voice delivering the test sentences. A month later the test was replicated with the same children in the same seating positions. On the second test application, the sentences were played with an identical level of test voice volume but with the addition of varying levels of background classroom noise. It was found that once background noise was introduced, the poorer readers in each class performed less effectively than their more able peers at identifying test sentences.

Bellamy - Listening Experiments

In an independent study, Bellamy and Long (1994), replicated the classroom listening measure with older students at a Community School in Wiltshire. They found a similar relationship existed between listening in background noise and spelling ability.

Recent Independent Studies

A report from the Royal National Institute for the Deaf (RNID 2006) reinforces the earlier 1980-2000 A.R.R.O.W. work into listening skills. The RNID believes that poor listening skills are affecting more than a million school children. The recent report's listening deficit findings for children were discovered when analysing results, drawn from a telephone hearing check. The data showed that, from a self-selecting sample of over 2000 children aged 10-14, one in five were unable to distinguish speech in noise at a level normally expected of adults. These children register as having hearing levels below normal, not because of problems with their ears, but due to a cognitive inability to distinguish sounds clearly in noisy environments. The report suggests that improved acoustics within a school and installation of effective sound systems for teachers and pupils would be a positive way of attacking the problem for pupils with poor listening skills.

Another investigation into listening skills has recently been conducted by Northwestern University, Illinois and confirms the relationship between listening in noise and literacy skills. Their research is reported in the university publication Newscenter Dec.07, 2009. Good and poor readers were asked to watch a video while the speech sound "da" was presented to them through an earphone in two different sessions, during which, the brain's responses to these sounds was continuously measured.

The good readers, 'tuned in' to the repeatedly presented speech sound context, more effectively than the poorer readers and sharpened the sound's encoding. In an additional session, the experimenters found that the, 'tuned in' good readers, with a more effective adaptive auditory system, performed better than poorer readers on perceiving speech when asked to repeat sentences against background noise. In parallel with the RNID findings, they also suggest improved sound systems and placement near a teacher would help improve the poor listeners' performance.

N.B. An important point needs to be made. A.R.R.O.W. research conducted since 1975, has shown that listening in less-than-ideal environments, is a skill which can be further improved through training. Whilst the improvement of acoustic environments and placement of a poor listener close to a teacher or speaker is very beneficial, there is a clear need to accept that auditory training also has a key role to play for many students and certainly for Hearing Impaired Pupils. Evidence from earlier A.R.R.O.W. studies in 1976 and indeed just after 1996, showed that children can further improve their listening skills within a noisy environment after a few hours of commencing A.R.R.O.W.

The Improvement of Listening Skills with School Age Students
See Appendix 37
The concerns regarding poor listening skills and how to improve them were addressed by A.R.R.O.W. in the 1996 Bridgwater project (Lane 2010). The study investigated the interrelationship of A.R.R.O.W. training upon the reading, spelling

and listening skills of children with literacy problems. A Junior School in Bridgwater, Somerset, was selected on the basis of having an acknowledged literacy problem. An opportunity sample of 21 pupils:- 19 boys and 2 girls (mean age 9.1 years), received A.R.R.O.W. training as a result of their poor literacy skills.

It was decided to evaluate the performance of the children in an A-B, B-C design, across two 5 week periods. The first period measured the childrens' progress in the school, using the mainstream and specialist help then available. The second period B-C, measured the childrens' A.R.R.O.W. progress using the same specialist staff and time allocation as for the first intervention. Tests for literacy and listening would be given to the children at points A, B and C.

Two reading tests were administered - the Schonell Word Reading Test and The Salford (B) Sentence Reading Test. The children were therefore, assessed on individual word recognition and contextual reading skills. The Schonell Graded Spelling Test was used to measure movement in spelling performances across the control and intervention periods.

The Teaching Methods during the Pre-A.R.R.O.W. Control Period
Prior to A.R.R.O.W. the pupils had been receiving structured multi-sensory teaching from a specialist teacher, plus a team of three full-time Teaching Assistants. The specialist teacher saw the students in groups, three times a week, and left support programs for the teaching assistants to follow for the remaining two days. In total, students received no more than two hours tuition per week.

A.R.R.O.W. Intervention Period Results
In the A.R.R.O.W. intervention 5 week period, standard A.R.R.O.W. programs were given by the same teacher and/or teaching assistants. Care was taken to ensure that the children received the equivalent amount of training time for the periods A-B and B-C.

Results showed a marked superiority after A.R.R.O.W. intervention compared to the control period.

Table 1: The Results of A.R.R.O.W. Intervention
A.R.R.O.W. results now being gained some twenty years after this study, reveal far greater literacy skill improvements with students. It should nevertheless, be noted that results from all four tests implemented during the Bridgwater project, revealed that the staff at the school achieved between 3-7 more times progress when using A.R.R.O.W. for reading, spelling and listening, than previously and that the differences were statistically significant.

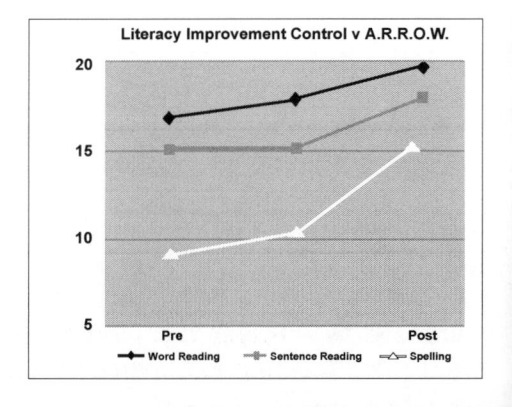

Chapter 10 - Listening Skill Improvements

	A–B period		B–C period	
Word Reading	improvement	1 month (6%)	improvement	3 months (17.6%)
Sentence Reading	improvement	0 month (0%)	improvement	3 months (23%)
Spelling Test	improvement	1 month (12.5%)	improvement	7 months (77%)

The Classroom Listening Test

As noted with reference to the Middle School experiment, The Classroom Listening Test requires a student to write down twenty short sentences or questions heard from an audio player, with the test voice gradually being lowered, whilst the background noise is increased. In the Bridgwater study, the pupils always sat between 3-4 metres from the tape player and occupied the same seating position throughout the three test applications. The children were encouraged to write down the words or sentences they heard, irrespective of their ability to spell these correctly. It was decided to measure:

1. The number of correctly identified words.
2. The number of words attempted.
3. The number of correctly spelt words.

It was found that there was an improvement in all three of the above points after undertaking A.R.R.O.W with the number of words correctly identified rising by 94%. The results confirmed previous A.R.R.O.W. findings that A.R.R.O.W. Self-Voice training improves the skill of listening to another voice against background noise. It is noted however, that listening skill score movement within the non-A.R.R.O.W. control period was negligible.

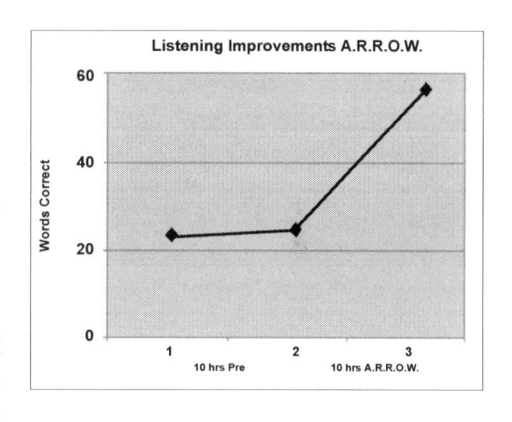

Suffolk Project – An Independent Study

In 1998, John Sanham, Senior Teacher of the Deaf, Suffolk, looked at the improvement of listening skills using A.R.R.O.W. with Year 1 pupils. The information is taken from his 1998 report to Suffolk Local Education Authority which was later submitted as part of his A.R.R.O.W. report. Twenty four children were involved in the project and were randomly selected. Twelve children formed the target A.R.R.O.W. Training Group, whilst another 12 formed the non-training in A.R.R.O.W. Control Group. A.R.R.O.W. Listening Training was given to the Target Group and consisted of 10 sessions of approximately 15 minutes each, i.e. a total training time of 2½ hours. The Control Group received no A.R.R.O.W. training. It is noteworthy that skill retention of the A.R.R.O.W. cohort was maintained 6-8 weeks after the cessation of training.

Sanham reports... *"The training was a procedure known as the A.R.R.O.W. Listening Training developed by Dr Colin Lane. The procedure is briefly as follows:*

A twenty sentence test is administered consisting of listening to a voice against increasing levels of background noise. After the initial test a recording was made of the child reading A.R.R.O.W. texts. The training program was then given which consists of intense listening to the Self-Voice against varying levels of background noise initially with access to the text but later purely by audition. As indicated the children were re-tested between six and eight weeks after the training sessions finished. The results were discussed within the report." and Sanham concludes:

"Clearly the greatest impact of the Listening Training was upon the Listening Test itself. The percentage shift for the Target Group was 18.5% whereas the Control Group's improvement was below 1%. ... the Listening Training given does seem to have a generally positive effect on reading, spelling and phonological abilities."

Listening Improvements with Hearing Impaired Adults

Encouraged by the early successful work with Hearing Impaired pupils, A.R.R.O.W. training was applied to selected adults with Hearing Impairment. Foremost of these adults, was a Teacher of Lipreading, who herself had a marked bi-lateral hearing loss. Her experiences proved inspirational to the development of A.R.R.O.W. Listening Training with Hearing Impaired adults.

She writes:
"I am a Teacher of Lipreading and wear two hearing aids. I became more hard of hearing as life went on and dropped out of my social life because of background noise etc. I could not hear any sound which was out of the room, round a corner, or in an 'Echoing' place. I could not speak with anyone unless it was full face to face with 100% Lipreading. Life was becoming a terrible strain. Then I got to know about A.R.R.O.W. I followed a prescribed training technique...I felt as if a piece of cotton wool had been teased out of a point above my forehead. I can hear sounds I never thought to pick up in this life again. Listening is not hearing and it is trainable – as proven to me personally. A colleague said she felt as if her ears had been exercised – a good way of putting it."

A 54 year old male adult acquired a hearing loss at the age of 48 years and was forced to retire from his post as a BBC Programmes Organiser. He writes of the improvement in his life style within a week of following A.R.R.O.W. Listening Training.

A personal (non-expert) viewpoint.
"After about six years of quite serious deafness, I joined in the A.R.R.O.W. scheme. I had one week of intensive exercise using the 'Self-Voice' language laboratory at home, several times a day. I believe my perception of sound was immediately improved:-

1. I could easily recognise my own voice, perfectly clearly, either on headphones or on a loudspeaker.
2. I could hear and recognize the same spoken passage in another voice with no difficulty.
3. (With perhaps a new found confidence), I could unscramble the noise in my hearing aid. Instead of simply a very loud cacophony, I could discern the sound of church bells; I could hear some birdsong (very precious); I could detect an unseen voice calling my name; even (tentatively) the possibility of a conversation with someone in a noisy crowded room; I was encouraged again to try and listen to Mozart!

I suppose my lifetime's career has been spent dealing in 'noise' and I have inevitable a bank of sound memories, which is now being unlocked. On its own, memory is a faulty and unreliable thing: I should be able to hear in my head the cry of a curlew, or the opening bars of the Emperor piano concerto (indeed, the whole of it), but in six years it has become more difficult, more vague. Now I think my perception, my awareness, is sharpening. Last week someone asked me if I could hear a distant owl hooting. I listened, and "Yes!" I could hear it. My doctor told me that my hearing would never improve. Perhaps my use of what I do hear, my listening is improving."

Listening Improvements and Career Progress
Following her experiences as a student using A.R.R.O.W., Joan Pinder began to deliver A.R.R.O.W. training with other students:

"As a severely Hearing Impaired adult, A.R.R.O.W. was a tremendous aid for the improvement of my listening skills. Following my personal experiences undertaking A.R.R.O.W. training, I applied A.R.R.O.W. with many hearing and Hearing Impaired adults with astonishing success. As a Weston College tutor and Teacher of Lipreading, I presented the A.R.R.O.W. programs to students of all ages and abilities who were experiencing reading, spelling and/or listening and speech problems. The A.R.R.O.W. programs proved over and over again that all students could be helped in a quick and efficient manner. The students' improvements led to improved self-esteem along with incredibly improved literacy and listening skills. Some College students were highly motivated and usually required a short burst of A.R.R.O.W. intervention whilst the 'plodders' or *'not interested'* pupils showed results even after 3-4 hours. Special Needs students used the programs to suit their individual needs, everyone a winner! I very much liked the careful yet intense preparation which had gone into the program and this negated the need for planning on my part. A surprise OFSTED visit to the college gave A.R.R.O.W. the highest possible grade mark."

The Bridlington Experiment

Another example of the impact of A.R.R.O.W. upon a Hearing Impaired adult's listening skills was given in 'Speech and language Therapy in Practice' – Winter 2002. In late August 2002, a small group of Normally Hearing students (n=6) in Bridlington, Yorkshire, were given the Background Noise Listening Test. Five of the students were re-tested within one hour without receiving any A.R.R.O.W. Listening Training. Mean scores on the initial test realised 60.6 words correct from 100 words contained within 20 sentences. Re-test scores averaged 65.2 words correct, an improvement of 7.59% against the original score. A sixth student was tested within the original group but was then given A.R.R.O.W. Listening Training. On re-test within the non-A.R.R.O.W. group, his score rose from a pre-training 51 to 82 correct after A.R.R.O.W. This represents an improvement of 60.78% against his original score and resulted in him moving from being the poorest, to the best, listener in the group. He comments:

"After completing the A.R.R.O.W. Listening Programs that took me approximately 25 minutes, I experienced a mental clarity, I had a feeling of heightened awareness, found it easier to focus on the voice and differentiate and exclude background noise."

The Listening Test and training programs were finally transferred from an audio cassette analogue format to DVD in 2009. A.R.R.O.W. immediately showed that it had not lost any of its impact as a result of the transition.

Listening Improvements with Normally Hearing Adults

In experiments conducted in Eire and England during Autumn/early Spring 2009, a selection of 56 trainee tutors were given the Listening Test within independent groups not exceeding 7 persons. Each group attended a different site when undertaking training, but all were positioned some 3-4 metres from external speakers during testing. An obtrusive level of background noise was introduced which, for some adults, masked the test voice.

Training procedures required the tutors to record an Advanced Level Topic. The tutors then followed a set of procedures in which they listened back to the Self-Voice under several conditions:

1. Using a very quiet level for the Self-Voice.
2. Introducing background noise to almost mask the Self-Voice recording.
3. Undertaking the listening to the Self-Voice against a selection of background noises.

After no more than 30 minutes self-training, the tutors were re-tested on the same assessment material. Results were extremely encouraging. Initial pre-training scores for the 56 trainee tutors averaged 45.10 from a total of 100 words within the 20 test sentences. After training average scores rose to 56.59, a relative improvement of 25.47%.

Results and tutors' comments previously quoted, attest to the efficacy of the approach. The lowest original score tutor from the opportunity sample of 56, moved from a score of 22 words identified to 47 on re-test, well over a 100% improvement. The lady tutor had a history of hearing problems and was extremely gratified with her improvement.

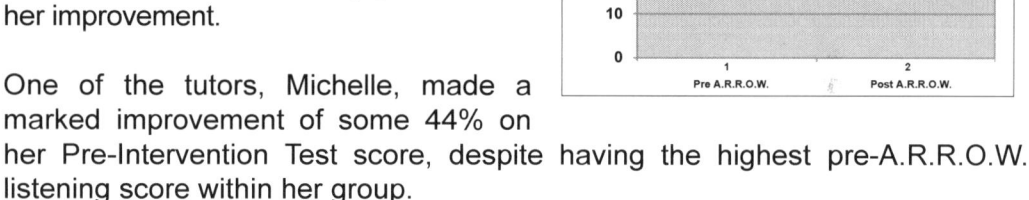

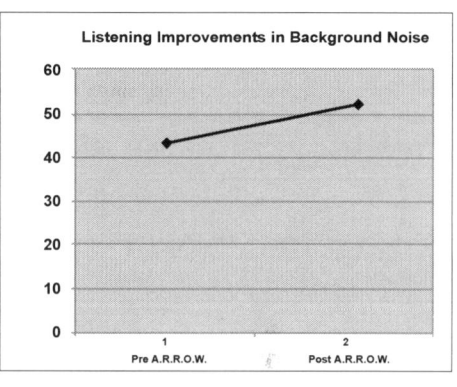

One of the tutors, Michelle, made a marked improvement of some 44% on her Pre-Intervention Test score, despite having the highest pre-A.R.R.O.W. listening score within her group.

She writes:
"Initially, I found the listening test much more difficult than I anticipated. In hindsight I was probably lacking in concentration e.g. my mind was awash with other issues that I needed to address during the day. I was also aware of how others were reacting. Subconsciously, I found myself trying to decipher the background noise as well as the voice, which caused some confusion. By the end of the test, I had lost all logic as to whether or not what I had written actually made sense. After undertaking training using various background noises the test appeared much easier. I was able to focus on the speech more. Although some words were still incoherent, I felt more confident at making an educated guess by using the words that I had heard. I'm not sure why but I was also less distracted by those around me."

Another tutor was asked to explain why she was able to improve from an easily worst-in-her-group level, to that achieved by some of the other tutors. Her response is self-explanatory:
"I tried harder"

Listening Improvements – Adults with Communication Problems
The adults undertaking the 'Your Skills' program have recently been assessed for listening in background noise performance before and after the A.R.R.O.W. 'Your Skills' program. The adult and tutor sat on the computer and listened to the background noise listening test through headsets. The test followed an audiometric format in which:

1. A series of successful responses by the student would result in the tutor lowering the voice but maintaining or raising the background noise.
2. A series of unsuccessful responses would result in the tutor raising the voice level and maintaining or lowering the background noise.
3. The abilities of adults varied considerably. The lowest adult score was 15, the highest was 87 with an average of 55 for the 32 participating students and a Standard Deviation of 21.83.

Some tutors occasionally let their adults meet specific background noise training itself, as part of their overall 'Your Skills' A.R.R.O.W. training program. Other tutors relied on the more usual form of A.R.R.O.W. Self-Voice work in order to raise listening standards.

Results were extremely encouraging. The 32 adults raised their average scores from 55 to 64, an improvement of 16.36%. Of particular interest were the results for 8 CVA adults whose averages rose from 57.75 to 73.5 an improvement of 27.27%. The marked rise in scores fits an overall A.R.R.O.W. listening pattern whereby both children and adults have improved their ability to listen in noise after A.R.R.O.W. using either:

1. The standard Self-Voice approach or
2. The more rapid and specific Listening in Background Noise training schedule.

Discussion
It seems clear that two components of listening are affected by A.R.R.O.W. Training. The first component is a subject's conscious awareness of both the need and capability to attend more diligently in auditory attention tasks. This was first realised in the 1980 A.R.R.O.W. Listening Project, with improvements in Environment Sound Identification, Sentence Understanding, Consonant Discrimination and Short Term Memory tasks for Digit and Word Recall. It is also later evident in the Suffolk project conducted with young pupils by John Sanham in Suffolk and by Hearing Impaired Adults and Trainee A.R.R.O.W. Tutors.

The second component is more difficult to define, but is in some way reflected in subliminal listening and sound detection. Adults report increasing awareness of environment sounds and speech detection in noise, following A.R.R.O.W. Listening Training. These life skill enhancements based upon improved environment and speech sound perception, have in some cases been realised without the adult consciously effecting a change in attitude when attempting to detect speech in less-than-ideal conditions.

Non verbal training to improve speech perception in noise
A 2017 report in Current Biology confirms earlier work by Bang which shows non-verbal training using pure tone pitch shift discrimination tasks, can lead to improved listening in noise speech perception. the length of time for non-verbal training to generalise to speech perception in noise in both studies is measured

in months rather than the one - four hour training schedule using A.R.R.O.W. Self-Voice.

Chapter 10 Conclusion

The demise of listening as a communication skill is noted and examples are given showing the pre-eminence of listening, the lost art, both at home and school during the decades covering 1940 – 1970. As a class teacher in the 1960's, the author well remembers the prevalence of quietness in a working classroom and the later emergence of unacceptable noise levels within some school environments. People listen differently. Some people are good listeners, others are not. The author delivered a Listening in Noise Test to teachers and found that there could be as much as a 96% difference in word detection between the highest and lowest achievers in a group. Examples are given of adults in the work place learning to listen through noise and of Hearing Impaired Children being better at identifying their own voices than children without any form of hearing loss. An overall background to listening is given, where it is observed that listening is an acquired skill. The relationship between skill at listening in noise and reading and spelling ability was found in Primary age and Secondary age pupils in experiments conducted during the 1990's. In effect poor listeners in noise were amongst the lowest achievers in their groups for both reading and spelling. Two recent independent studies by the RNID in the UK and Northwestern University in the USA, confirm the earlier A.R.R.O.W. based studies. An A.R.R.O.W. project was conducted in a Somerset Primary school with 9 year old pupils. The pupils were experiencing severe literacy problems. It was found that under a 5 week control period little literacy progress was made by specialist staff and no progress occurred in listening in noise performances. After 5 weeks A.R.R.O.W. reading and spelling had improved by a factor of between 3 to 7 dependent upon which test was applied. Listening in noise skills however, improved by almost 100% when compared to the previous two applications. An independent listening training project was undertaken in Suffolk with Year 1 students and it was found that they improved their listening in noise skills by 18% one month after A.R.R.O.W. training ceased, whereas a control group failed to measure any improvement. Case studies are cited with hearing impaired adults in which lifestyles have changed through improvements in listening after A.R.R.O.W. A group experiment in Bridlington showed that the poorest listener in a group of adults became the best listener after A.R.R.O.W. Adults in Eire and England received A.R.R.O.W. Background Noise programs and improved their scores by 25.4% after 30 minutes training. Adults with communication problems on the 'Your Skills' program made a 16% improvement after the closure of their A.R.R.O.W. course. It seems apparent that two listening components are in action under A.R.R.O.W. The first is the subject's conscious ability to attend more diligently on listening tasks, the second is a more subliminal awareness of sound without the need to make a conscious effort when improving sound detection. The rapidity of A.R.R.O.W. Self-Voice auditory training compared to other strategies is noted.

Appendices

1. Environment Sound Test Results ... 149
2. Consonant Discrimination Test ... 149
3. Sentence Understanding Test ... 149
4. The Digit Recall Test ... 149
5. Word Recall Test ... 150
6. The Vocalisation Test - Action of Story ... 150
7. Self-Voice Recognition amongst Children - Sentence ... 150
8. Self-Voice Recognition amongst Children - Word List (Reverse Sentence) ... 150
9. Self-Voice Recognition amongst Children - Vowel ... 151
10. Voice Self-Esteem Measure © ... 151
11. Memory Recall Tasks using Self-Voice ... 152
12. Independent A.R.R.O.W. Research ... 152
13. Primary School improvements following maximum 10 hours A.R.R.O.W. ... 152
14. Primary School Devon. Results after 2-3 hours A.R.R.O.W. ... 153
15. Neale Analysis Reading Ability ... 153
17. English as an Additional Language at Home ... 153
18. Results after 2-3 hours A.R.R.O.W. Wigan Primary School ... 153
19. Results after 7+ hours A.R.R.O.W. Rhondda Valley Primary School ... 154
20. Secondary Schools/Colleges Improvements following maximum 10 hours A.R.R.O.W. ... 154
21. Results after 3-4 hours A.R.R.O.W. South West Community College ... 154
22. Stroke N = 39   1st Intervention ... 154

23. Stroke N = 30   2nd Intervention 155

24. The effects of further interventions 155

25. Residential Homes n = 30   1st Intervention 155

26. Residential Homes n = 19   2nd Intervention 156

27. Residential Homes n = 13   3rd Intervention 156

28. Learning Problem adults n = 228   1st Intervention 156

29. Learning Problem adults n = 166   2nd Intervention 156

30. Learning Problem adults n = 12   7th Intervention 157

31. Group 4 Headway - adults with brain injury n = 13   1st Intervention . . . 157

32. Group 4 Headway - adults with brain injury n = 13   2nd Intervention . . . 157

33. Group 4 Headway - adults with brain injury n = 13   4th Intervention . . . 158

34. Reading Skills 158

35. Spelling Skills 159

36. Two hour intervention 159

37. The Bridgwater Junior School results pre/post A.R.R.O.W. 160

38. Taunton Project Combined Reading/Spelling results in Yrs. 4, 5, 6 160

39. Taunton Project Two subgroups EAL & SEN 160

Appendices

1. Environment Sound Test Results
Student scores are shown for both the A-B non A.R.R.O.W. control period, and B-C. A.R.R.O.W. intervention period.

Students	Scores A	Scores B	%	Scores B	Scores C	%
23	201	199	-1	199	267	+ 34.17

2. Consonant Discrimination Test
Combined scores for non A.R.R.O.W. control period A-B and B-C. A.R.R.O.W. intervention period.

Pupils	Scores A	Scores B	%	Scores B	Scores C	%
23	324	348	+ 7.4	348	453	+ 30.17

3. Sentence Understanding Test
Combined scores for non A.R.R.O.W. control period A-B and B-C. A.R.R.O.W. intervention period.

Students	Scores A	Scores B	%	Scores B	Scores C	%
23	452	467	+ 3.31	467	639	+ 36.83

4. The Digit Recall Test
Combined scores for non A.R.R.O.W. control period A-B and B-C. A.R.R.O.W. intervention period.

Students	Scores A	Scores B	%	Scores B	Scores C	%
23	387	413	+ 6.71	413	483	+ 16.94

5. Word Recall Test
Combined scores for non A.R.R.O.W. control period A-B and B-C.
A.R.R.O.W. intervention period.

Students	Scores A	Scores B	%	Scores B	Scores C	%
23	287	299	+ 4.18	299	386	+ 29.09

6. The Vocalisation Test - Action of Story
Combined scores for non A.R.R.O.W. control period A-B and B-C.
A.R.R.O.W. intervention period.

Students	Scores A	Scores B	%	Scores B	Scores C	%
23	391	409	+ 4.60	409	568	+ 38.87

7. Self-Voice Recognition amongst Children - Sentence

% Correct Recognition			
Sentence	1-2 secs	11-15 secs	2-3 mins
High V.S.E.	80.5	84.2	88.8
Low V.S.E.	84.2	84.2	83.3
Hearing Impaired	89.4	89.4	78.9

8. Self-Voice Recognition amongst Children - Word List (Reverse Sentence)

% Correct Recognition			
Reverse	1-2 secs	11-15 secs	2-3 mins
High V.S.E.	87.0	88.8	89.8
Low V.S.E.	92.5	83.3	85.1
Hearing Impaired	94.7	89.4	57.8

9. Self-Voice Recognition amongst Children - Vowel

% Correct Recognition			
Vowel	1-2 secs	11-15 secs	2-3 mins
High V.S.E.	72.2	50.0	46.2
Low V.S.E.	71.2	44.0	45.3
Hearing Impaired	89.4	52.6	47.3

10. Voice Self-Esteem Measure ©

1. My friends like my voice.
2. I'm proud of my voice.
3. I'm ashamed of my voice.
4. I've got a lovely voice.
5. I think lots of people would like a voice like mine.
6. I like people to hear my voice.
7. Nobody wants a voice like mine.
8. My voice cheers people up.
9. Teacher asks me to read because my voice sounds good.
10. My voice is the worst in the world.
11. I love to hear my voice when it's recorded.
12. I like everyone to know what a nice voice I've got.
13. I like the sound of my voice.
14. I don't mind talking to a large audience.
15. I'm glad my voice is like it is.
16. My voice is the best in the world.
17. Everyone seems to like my voice.
18. Teachers say they like my voice.
19. My voice always sounds good.
20. My voice doesn't sound how I want it to.
21. My voice sounds right for my age.
22. I dislike my voice.

V.S.E. Mean 9.59   S.D. 4.05
108 children exhibited H.V.S.E.
108 children exhibited L.V.S.E.

11. Memory Recall Tasks using Self-Voice

Subject	1	2	3	4	5	6	7	8	9	10	11	12
Recalled Words	10	6	7	4	9	7	5	11	5	7	6	5
Self-Voice	7	4	7	2	5	4	3	7	3	5	3	2
Percentage	70	66	100	50	55	57	60	63	60	71	50	40

12. Independent A.R.R.O.W. Research

Year 6 Students n=85		
Pre A.R.R.O.W. Reading Age	Post A.R.R.O.W. Reading Age	Gains
11.92 years	13.28 years	1.36 years
Pre A.R.R.O.W. Spelling Age 11.06 years	Post A.R.R.O.W. Spelling Age 11.75 years	0.7 years
Pre A.R.R.O.W. Comprehension Age 10.39 years	Post A.R.R.O.W. Comprehension Age 12.27 years	1.88 years

13. Primary School improvements following maximum 10 hours A.R.R.O.W.

Students n = 779 Schools n = 35	Pre A.R.R.O.W. Average	Post A.R.R.O.W. Average	Gain Months Average
Reading	40.35	48.71	9
Spelling	34.63	38.7	5

14. Primary School Devon. Results after 2-3 hours A.R.R.O.W.

No. Students	Average age in yrs.	Reading Pre Average	Reading Post Average	Gain Mths. Average	Spelling Pre Average	Spelling Post Average	Gain Mths. Average
23	9.9 yrs.	39.43	45.04	6	35.52	38.17	4

15. Neale Analysis Reading Ability

Word Attack Pre	Word Attack Post	Gain Mths. Average	Comp Pre Average	Comp Post Average	Gain Mths. Average	Reading Rate Pre	Reading Rate Post	Gain Mths. Average
90.17	95.16	10.5	88	96.33	16.33	88.33	94.5	18.8

16. Weschler WORD Spelling Test

Spelling Pre Average	Spelling Post Average	Gain Mths. Average
89	90.71	4.71

17. English as an Additional Language at Home

No. Students	Age Average	Reading Pre Average	Reading Post Average	Gain Mths. Average	Spelling Pre Average	Spelling Post Average	Gain Mths. Average
6	9.9 yrs.	26.5	32.5	8	24.33	28	4

18. Results after 2-3 hours A.R.R.O.W. Wigan Primary School

No. Students	Age Average	Reading Pre Average	Reading Post Average	Gain Mths. Average	Spelling Pre Average	Spelling Post Average	Gain Mths. Average
30	10.8 yrs.	74.5	85.92	8	63.46	66.96	4

19. Results after 7+ hours A.R.R.O.W. Rhondda Valley Primary School

No. Students	Age Average	Reading Pre Average	Reading Post Average	Gain Mths. Average	Spelling Pre Average	Spelling Post Average	Gain Mths. Average
20	10.5 yrs.	56.4	80.9	29	48.75	62.25	14

20. Secondary Schools/Colleges Improvements following maximum 10 hours A.R.R.O.W.

Students n = 428 Schools n = 19	Pre A.R.R.O.W. Average	Post A.R.R.O.W. Average	Gain Months Average
Reading	47.72	57.49	8
Spelling	41.63	46.56	5

21. Results after 3-4 hours A.R.R.O.W. South West Community College

No. Students	Age Average	Reading Pre Average	Reading Post Average	Gain Mths. Average	Spelling Pre Average	Spelling Post Average	Gain Mths. Average
24	11.9 yrs.	44.73	54.78	9	34.87	38.41	4

22. Stroke N = 39 1st Intervention

Reading Pre Average	Reading Post Average	Spelling Pre Average	Spelling Post Average	Digit Pre Average	Digit Post Average	Word Pre Average	Word Post Average
66.00	71.54	31.46	38.67	25.46	27.74	17.31	19.59

23. Stroke N = 30 2nd Intervention

Reading Pre Average	Reading Post Average	Spelling Pre Average	Spelling Post Average	Digit Pre Average	Digit Post Average	Word Pre Average	Word Post Average
68.97	73.40	42.17	48.40	26.57	29.07	19.40	21.97

24. The effects of further interventions

CVA Interventions	No.	Reading Pre Average	Reading Post Average	Spelling Pre Average	Spelling Post Average	Digit Pre Average	Digit Post Average	Word Pre Average	Word Post Average
CVA 1st Intervention	12	62.75	69.08	27.42	33.42	25.50	28.17	18.17	20.17
CVA 2nd Intervention	12	63.92	68.25	38.50	44.58	26.33	28.42	18.75	20.50
CVA 3rd Intervention	12	64.41	70.5	44.25	51.08	25.83	27.58	18.58	19.83
CVA 4th Intervention	12	73.16	75.66	54.00	58.25	26.75	28.16	19.66	21.08
CVA 5th Intervention	12	75.41	77.4	57.50	61.33	27.16	29.00	20.18	21.63
CVA 6th Intervention	12	78.33	83.17	60.33	64.67	26.92	28.50	21.00	22.33

25. Residential Homes n = 30 1st Intervention

Reading Pre Average	Reading Post Average	Spelling Pre Average	Spelling Post Average	Digit Pre Average	Digit Post Average	Word Pre Average	Word Post Average
62.23	70.59	42.70	50.50	26.03	27.90	17.52	21.79

26. Residential Homes n = 19   2nd Intervention

Reading Pre Average	Reading Post Average	Spelling Pre Average	Spelling Post Average	Digit Pre Average	Digit Post Average	Word Pre Average	Word Post Average
69.37	71.11	64.00	67.32	28.32	29.68	22.47	23.37

27. Residential Homes n = 13   3rd Intervention

RH Interventions	No.	Reading Pre Average	Reading Post Average	Spelling Pre Average	Spelling Post Average	Digit Pre Average	Digit Post Average	Word Pre Average	Word Post Average
RH 1st Intervention	13	65.90	71.99	61.30	66.29	30.29	31.01	21.23	25.99
RH 2nd Intervention	13	80.84	83.30	62.16	66.48	30.65	31.26	24.99	28.94
RH 3rd Intervention	13	78.33	80.33	65.62	70.46	31.46	32.08	25.62	27.62

28. Learning Problem adults n = 228   1st Intervention

Reading Pre Average	Reading Post Average	Spelling Pre Average	Spelling Post Average	Digit Pre Average	Digit Post Average	Word Pre Average	Word Post Average
52.24	57.51	36.38	41.72	20.08	22.92	15.82	17.73

29. Learning Problem adults n = 166   2nd Intervention

Reading Pre Average	Reading Post Average	Spelling Pre Average	Spelling Post Average	Digit Pre Average	Digit Post Average	Word Pre Average	Word Post Average
56.40	61.13	40.44	45.01	21.19	23.05	16.46	19.17

30. Learning Problem adults n = 12   7th Intervention

SLP Interventions	No.	Reading Pre Average	Reading Post Average	Spelling Pre Average	Spelling Post Average	Digit Pre Average	Digit Post Average	Word Pre Average	Word Post Average
SLP 1st Intervention	12	34.08	42.9	22.08	26.9	20	22.08	15.75	16.91
SLP 2nd Intervention	12	41.58	48.5	25.58	27.33	20.66	22.75	15	17.41
SLP 3rd Intervention	12	45.41	50.16	21.75	27.91	20.08	22.41	18.41	18.66
SLP 4th Intervention	12	47.41	47.41	27.00	30.16	21.66	23.66	18.16	17.83
SLP 5th Intervention	12	49.91	55.16	27.00	28.75	22.00	22.91	17.41	17.25
SLP 6th Intervention	12	53.50	57.75	28.41	29.91	20.41	21.75	16.50	18.00
SLP 7th Intervention	12	51.75	56.33	27.83	29.83	23.16	23.16	17.58	17.50

31. Group 4 Headway - adults with brain injury n = 13   1st Intervention

Reading Pre Average	Reading Post Average	Spelling Pre Average	Spelling Post Average	Digit Pre Average	Digit Post Average	Word Pre Average	Word Post Average
64.46	70.69	40.92	48.92	24.46	27.92	17.46	19.92

32. Group 4 Headway - adults with brain injury n = 13   2nd Intervention

Reading Pre Average	Reading Post Average	Spelling Pre Average	Spelling Post Average	Digit Pre Average	Digit Post Average	Word Pre Average	Word Post Average
68.53	74.53	47.38	54.46	26.69	28.84	19.38	20.61

33. Group 4 Headway - adults with brain injury n = 13 4th Intervention

Brain Injured Interventions	No.	Reading Pre Average	Reading Post Average	Spelling Pre Average	Spelling Post Average	Digit Pre Average	Digit Post Average	Word Pre Average	Word Post Average
BI 1st Intervention	13	64.46	70.69	40.92	48.92	24.46	27.92	17.46	19.92
BI 2nd Intervention	13	68.53	74.53	47.38	54.46	26.69	28.84	19.38	20.61
BI 3rd Intervention	13	75.3	78.92	54.15	60.00	28.61	30.61	21.00	22.38
BI 4th Intervention	13	75.69	81.07	54.84	61.69	29.00	30.76	21.3	23.07

34. Reading Skills

Job Seeker n = 6	Pre A.R.R.O.W. Reading Score	Post A.R.R.O.W. Reading Score
L	71	80
S	73	84
J	35	44
C	25	31
R	12	18
Cal.	73	83
Average	48.16	56.66
Reading Age	9 yrs. 5 mths.	10 yrs. 1 mth.

35. Spelling Skills

Job Seeker n = 7	Pre A.R.R.O.W. Spelling Score	Post A.R.R.O.W. Spelling Score
D	15	22
L	20	34
S	60	72
R	4	9
C	10	22
CA	60	63
R	19	24
Average	26.85	35.14
Spelling Age	7 yrs. 8 mths.	8 yrs. 6 mths.

36. Two hour intervention

Exeter Intervention	Pre Reading	Post Reading	Pre Spelling	Post Spelling
BB	47	55	34	36
BR	63	75	41	46
FG	64	67	36	40
G	36	44	12	14
HS	74	84	62	69
HR	43	46	26	29
HM	63	70	43	49
LL	71	81	42	49
ML	79	86	75	77
RF	19	22	20	18
WR	88	88	64	63
	58.81	65.27	41.36	44.54
Ability Age	10 yrs. 2 mths.	10 yrs. 8 mths.	9 yrs. 2 mths.	9 yrs. 6 mths.

The table shows that the least able student scored at a level of 7 years 3 months in terms of reading ability. The least able speller scored at a level of 6 years and 3 months.

37. The Bridgwater Junior School results pre/post A.R.R.O.W.

	5 week control		5 week A.R.R.O.W.	
	A	B	B	C
Schonell Word Reading Test	6y 6m	6y 7m	6y 7m	6y 10m
Salford Sentences Reading Test	6y 4m	6y 4m	6y 4m	6y 7m
Schonell Spelling Test	5y 8m	5y 9m	5y 9m	6y 4m
Classroom Listening Test Word Count Correct	26.18	26.85	26.85	52.00
Classroom Listening Test Correct Spellings	28.38	28.40	28.40	48.4

38. Taunton Project Combined Reading/Spelling results in Yrs. 4, 5, 6

Total Students = 18	Pre A.R.R.O.W. Average Scores	Post A.R.R.O.W. Average Scores	Gain in Months
Reading (n=17)	55.76	65.29	9m
Spelling (n=18)	44.22	51.83	9m

39. Taunton Project Two subgroups EAL & SEN

EAL Total Students (n=7)	Pre A.R.R.O.W. Scores	Post A.R.R.O.W. Scores	Gain in Months
Reading	52.87	63.62	10m
Spelling	43.93	51.18	8m

SEN Total Students (n=6)	Pre A.R.R.O.W. Scores	Post A.R.R.O.W. Scores	Gain in Months
Reading	54.65	63.2	7m
Spelling	40.83	48.8	9m

References

Bang, C. (2008) A World of Sound and Music online multimedia documentation. Aalborg University and Edvantage group.

Bellamy, H. and Long, L. (1994) In: Lane, C.H. A.R.R.O.W. links 2(3) 5-9.

Boder, E. and Jarrico, S. (1982) The Boder test of reading and spelling patterns. New York, Grune and Stratton.

British Society of Audiology (2011) Positon Statement Auditory Processing Disorder (APD).

Brooks, G. and NFER (2007) What works for pupils with literacy difficulties. Department for children, schools and families.

Chivers, M. (2004) Practical Strategies for Living with Dyslexia. Jessica Kingsley Publishers London and Philadelphia pp 37-42.

Cole, J.F. (1995) Personal Communication.

Conrad, R. (1979) The Deaf School Child. Harper and Row. London.

Copeland, R.H. (1960) The Effects of Free-field Feedback Modification on Verbal Behaviour. Paper presented to the Amer. Speech Hear Assoc. Los Angeles.1960 In: Ellis, N.R. Handbook of Mental Deficiency 1963.

Crewdson, D. (1996) The sound of one's voice. RCSLT Bulletin Sept.1996 Issue 553 pp. 8-9.

Current Biology, (2017) Volume 27 Issue 21, pp 3237-3247.

Goddard, S. (1996) A Teacher's Window into the Child's Mind. Fern Ridge Press pp 82-3.

Gross, J. (2009) News Centre Dcsf 15th Oct. 2009.

Houston, J. (Report on work conducted Hertfordshire 1996 - 2001).

Knight, P. (2010) Interview Treorci.

Lane, C.H. (1975) Programming Techniques for Hearing Impaired Children.

The Journal of the Society of Teachers of the Deaf .20. pp. 17-21.

Lane, C.H. (1976) ARROW Talk Spring 1976 79. National Deaf Children's Society. pp. 19-21.

Lane, C.H. (1978) The "Arrow" Approach for Aural Rehabilitation. The Volta Review. 80 pp. 149-154.

Lane, C.H. (1980) The Improvement of Listening and Speech Skills in Language Disordered Children. Unpublished M.Ed dissertation. Univ. Exeter.

Lane, C.H. (1986) Various Aspects of Voice Self-Concept amongst Normally Hearing and Hearing-Impaired Children. Unpublished Ph.D. Thesis, Univ. Exeter.

Lane, C.H. (1990) ARROW: Alleviating Children's Reading and Spelling Difficulties In: Pumfrey P.D. and Elliott C.D. Children's Difficulties in Reading, Spelling and Writing, The Falmer Press Lewes pp. 237-254.

Lane, C.H. (1999) Report to Liverpool Dysphasia Support Group University Hospital Aintree. A.R.R.O.W. Tuition.

Lane, C.H. (2002) Speech and Language Therapy in Practice Winter 2002. pp. 26 27.

Lane, C.H. (2005) The Arrow Approach for Dyslexic Learners. The Dyslexia Handbook Ed: Tresman, S and Cooke, A. British Dyslexia Association. pp. 304-309

Lane, C.H. (2010) The A.R.R.O.W. Manual. A.R.R.O.W. Tuition Bridgwater Somerset.

Lane, C.H. and Chinn, S.J. (1986) Learning by Self-Voice Echo. Academic Therapy 21:4 pp. 477-481.

Martin, G.B. and Clark, R.D. (1982) Distress crying in neonates-species and peer specificity. Developmental Psychology. 18,1, pp. 3-9.

McCarthy, J.J. and Kirk, S.A. (1961) Examiners Manual I.T.P.A. Illinois Institute for Research on Exceptional Children. Urbana. Illinois University of Illinois Press.

Mcleod, F.J. MacMillan, P. Norwich, B. (2008) 'Listening to myself:

improving oracy and literacy among children who fall behind'. Early Child Development and Care. 177:6, pp. 633-644.

Neale, M.D. (1999) Neale Analysis of reading ability: manual (3rd edn) Melbourne, Australian Council for Educational Research.

Northwestern University Illinois Newscenter Dec 7th 2009.

Nugent, M. (2012) ARROW: A New Tool in the Teaching of Literacy: Report of Early Evaluation REACH Journal of Special Needs Education in Ireland,Vol.25 No.2 (2012).

Parsons, J. (2008) Interview Lyme Regis.

Reed, M. (1970) Hearing Test Cards. London.
Reynell, J. (1969) Developmental Language Scales RDLS Examiner's Manual.

Rousey, C. and Holzman, P.S. (1967) Recognition of One's Own Voice. J.Personality and Social Psychol. 6, 4. pp. 464-466.

Royal National Institute for the Deaf (2006) 'Breaking the Sound Barrier' Telephone Hearing Check www.breakingthesoundbarrier.org.uk

Salford Sentence Reading Test G.E. Bookbinder. Hodder and Stoughton.

Schonell graded word reading test: 1976 Aston Index LDA.

Vile, J. (1998) Unpublished Dissertation. University of Surrey.

Waldon, E.F. "The Baby Cry Test" In: Report of the Proceedings of the International Congress on the Education of the Deaf. Washington D.C. U.S. Gov. Printing Office, 1964. pp. 599-603 In: Bender, R.E. 185-6 The Conquest of Deafness. 1970.

Walton, K. (1985) Interview Burnham on Sea.

Wechsler, D. (1993) Weschler Objective Reading Dimensions (WORD). London: The Psychological Corporation.

Whitton, J.P. Hancock, K.E. Shannon, J.M. Polley, D.B. (2017) Audio Motor Perceptual Training Enhances Speech Intelligibility in Background Noise Current Biology, Volume 27, Issue 21. 2017. pp 3237-3247.

Index

A

A.R.R.O.W.
- Defined 1
- Economic Advantages of Using A.R.R.O.W. 17
- Equipment
  - Audio Cassette Recorder 58
  - Cine Projector - Cartoon 16
  - Disadvantages of Audio Cassette 59
  - DVD Emergence of Computer Technology 59
  - Headphones 8
  - Mirror and Tactile Teaching 14
  - Reel to Reel Dual Track Recorders 8
  - Visual Display System 17
- Origins 7
- Tutors
  - The Bridgwater College 'Your Skills' A.R.R.O.W. Tutors 104
  - Trainer of Tutors Course 65
  - Tutor Training Procedures 89
  - Tutors, Format of Tutor Training Program 65
Alphabet 62

B

Background Noise Listening Improvements
- Bridlington Experiment into Listening Skills 142
- Listening Improvements Adults with Communication Problems 143
- Listening Improvements with Normally Hearing Adults 142
- Suffolk Project – An Independent Study 139
- The Classroom Listening Test 139
- The Improvement of Listening Skills with School Age Students - Bridgwater Project (Lane 2010) ... 137
Basic Skills Assessments/Arrow Assessments 123

C

Cascading A.R.R.O.W. - Procedures Failure of Cascading 58
Case Studies
- Adult Distance Learning UK 91
- Adult Distance Learning USA 90
- Adult with Alzheimer's 99
- Adults with Stroke 97, 107
- Distance Learning Boy - Case Study 2 87
- Distance Learning Girl - Case Study 1 86
- Hearing Impaired Pupil - Case Study 18
Cassette Recorders - The Use of a Tutor and Single Cassette Recorder 58
Chanting 56
Coloured Background 60

Comprehension
    Comprehension Skills 69
    Independent A.R.R.O.W. Research 69

D

Differentiation and Pupil Needs - South West Primary School 74
Differentiation and Score Measurement - Adults in the Community 106
Digit Recall 26, 107, 112-117
Distance Learning
    Adult Distance Learning - UK 91
    Adult Distance Learning - USA 90
    Distance Learning Boy - Case Study 2 87
    Distance Learning Girl - Case Study 1 86
    Distance Learning Parent from Ireland 88
    Religious Group 89
Driving Test Program Customised - Job Seekers 122

E

Echoic Storage of the Self-Voice 44
Echoing 11
    Echoing - A Justification 39
    Echoing and Split Record during Clinical Practice - Example 1 12
    Echoing and Split Record during Clinical Practice - Example 2 12
English as an Additional Language at Home 76

F

Flexibility of A.R.R.O.W.
    Distance Learning
        Adult Distance Learning - UK 91
        Adult Distance Learning - USA 90
        Distance Learning Boy - Case Study 2 87
        Distance Learning Girl - Case Study 1 86
        Distance Learning Parent from Ireland 88
        Religious Group 89
    Eire 70, 85
    Free Field A.R.R.O.W. DVD Pre-Reader / Free Field Techniques 61
    Organisation of One Week Intervention 73, 80
    Student Centred Language 61
    The West Indies Pattern 84
    Timescales Used for Application 64

G

General Self-Esteem 40
Grammatical Error Work 61
Groundbreaking Evidence Years 1 and 2 72

H

Hearing
- Hearing a Faculty ... 135
- Hearing Impaired Children
  - A.R.R.O.W. The Origins ... 7
  - Case Study ... 18
  - Early Listening and Speech Research ... 22-30
  - Hearing Impaired Children ... 36
  - Hearing Impaired Voices ... 35
  - Pre-A.R.R.O.W. Speech and Language Improvement Strategies ... 9
  - Pupils' Reaction and Impact of A.R.R.O.W. ... 11
  - Research into the Self-Voice ... 32-41
  - Speech and Articulation Therapy ... 14
- Listening Improvements - Hearing Impaired Adults ... 140
- Listening Improvements and Career Progress ... 141

I

Internal Speech
- Defined - The Self-Voice and Internal Speech Some Considerations ... 44
- Internal Speech and the Self-Voice - A Running Dialogue ... 50
- Interrelationship between Literacy Skills and Internal Speech ... 45, 46
- Mental Lexicon ... 44
- Phonological Coding - The Somerset Experiment ... 46
  - Effects of A.R.R.O.W. upon Working Short Term Memory Visually Dominant Children ... 47, 48
- Short Term Memory - Residential Home - 2 Interventions ... 112
  - Digit/Word Recall ... 112
- Short Term Memory - Severe Learning Problem Adults - 7 Interventions ... 115
  - Digit/Word Recall ... 115
- Short Term Memory - Stroke - 3 Interventions ... 107
  - Digit/Word Recall ... 107
- Short Term Memory Gains
  - Digit Recall Test ... 26
  - Word Recall Test ... 26
- Short Term Memory Headway - Adults Brain Injury - 4 Interventions ... 117
  - Digit/Word Recall ... 117
- Spelling and Internal Speech Processes ... 46

J

Junior School - Listening a Lost Art ... 134
Junior School Use of Tape Recorders - On First Meeting the Recorded Self-Voice ... 6

K

Keene, M - National Behaviour Support Service Eire ... 86
Knight, P - The Self-Voice Experience Prior to Recorded Voice Playback ... 6

L

Leicester Pilot Project 76
Listening
    Bellamy Listening Experiments 136
    Early Listening and Speech Research 22-30
        Listening Range 23
            Comfortable Listening Level 23
            Correct/Incorrect Response Procedures 23
            Quiet Listening Level 23
        The Research Design 22
            Test Battery 22
                Consonant Discrimination Test 25
                Digit Recall Test 26
                Sentence Understanding Test 25
                The Environment Sound Test 24
                Word Recall Test 26
        Training 22
    Effects of Background Noise on Listening/Literacy Skills 136
    Lane - Listening and Literacy Experiments 136
    Learning to Listen 135
    Listening - A Lost Art 134
    Listening Classroom Listening Test 139
    Listening Differences 135
    Listening Improvements – Adults with Communication Problems 143
    Listening Improvements and Career Progress 141
    Listening Improvements with Hearing Impaired Adults 140
    Listening Improvements with Normally Hearing Adults 142
    Non verbal training to improve speech perception in noise 144
    Recent Independent Studies 137
    Relationship between Literacy Deficit and Listening Skills 136
    The Bridlington Experiment 142
    The Improvement of Listening Skills with School Age Students 137
    The Listening Range 23
        Comfortable Listening Level 23
        Evidence Regarding the Listening Range 28
        Listening Range Summary of Findings 28
        Quiet Listening Level 23
Literacy Improvements
    A.R.R.O.W. Reading and Spelling Improvements Primary Schools 72-78
        Groundbreaking Evidence Years 1 and 2 72
        Primary School South West - Results after 2-3 hours 73-76
            Additional Tests 74
            Comprehension Skills 75
            Differentiation and Pupil Needs 74
            English as an Additional Language at Home 76
            Neale Analysis Reading Ability 75
            Organisation of the One Week Intervention 73
            Pre-intervention Performance for Reading and Spelling 73
            Spelling Control Group 74
            Weschler WORD Spelling Test 75
        Results 72, 78
    A.R.R.O.W. Reading and Spelling Improvements Secondary Schools/Colleges 78-81
        A.R.R.O.W. Intervention at a South West Community College 79
        Differentiation and Pupil Needs 80
        Organisation of One Week Intervention 80

Index

    Pre-intervention Performance for Reading and Spelling 80
    Results after 3-4 Hours A.R.R.O.W. 80
Accepted Effectiveness - Departmental Approval 69
Independent A.R.R.O.W. Research 69
    Results 69
Literacy Improvements with Average/Above Average Pupils
    Rhondda Valley 78
    Trinidad - Above Average 85
    Wigan 77
Non-A.R.R.O.W. Self-Voice Study - Word Recognition Improvements 70
Rapid Learning Two Hour Exeter Project 129-131
    Adults Self-Assessment of Progress 131
    Results 130
    Student Selection 129
Reading and Spelling Skill Gains - Adults in the Community 107-118
    Reading/Spelling Headway - Adults Brain Injury - 4 Interventions 117
    Reading/Spelling Residential Homes - 2 Interventions 112
    Reading/Spelling Severe Learning Problem - 7 Interventions 115
    Reading/Spelling Stroke - 3 Interventions 107
Reading Skills Job Seekers - Results 125
Spelling Skills Job Seekers - Results 125
The Taunton Project 2017 78

M

Materials and Contents
    Audio Cassette 58
    DVD Material 61
        Alphabet 62
    Early Materials 15
    Poetry 16, 57
    Reading and Spellings
        Curriculum Based Spellings Free Field Facility 64
        Graded Spelling Programs 62
        High Ability Level Spellings 63
        High and Medium Frequency Words 63
        Personal Spelling Profile System 63
        Spelling Rules 64
        Topics 60
        Topics - Non Access to Text When Recording 61
    Spelling 16, 58
Meningitis 101
Multiplication Table Rote Learning through Self-Voice Echo 48

N

Need for Tutor Training 58
Normally Hearing Adults Listening Improvements 142

O

Organisation of 2-3 hr One Week Intervention - South West Primary School 73
Organisation of One Week Intervention - South West College 80
Other's Findings - Speech Clinicians and Self-Voice 9

P

Parent Positive Attitudes 10, 87
Personal Spelling Profile System 63
Pitch Range 39
Poetry 16
Pre-intervention Performance for Reading and Spelling 73, 80
Procedures A.R.R.O.W.
    Early Speech Procedures 14
    Traditional one to one Speech Procedure 14
Pupils' Reaction and Impact of A.R.R.O.W. 11

Q

Questions 105
Quiet Listening Level 23

R

Reading - Spelling Programs
    Alphabet 62
    Curriculum Based Spellings - Free Field Facility 64
    Differentiation 74, 106
    Early text book and tapes 15
    Free Writing Following Self-Voice Dictation 105
    Grammatical Error Work 61
    High Ability Spellings 63
    High Frequency Words 63
    Medium Frequency Words 63
    Personal Spelling Profile 63
    Poetry 16, 57
    Pre-Reading Skill Acquisition 55
    Spelling Rules 64
    Spellings 16, 62, 105
    Survival Words 105
    Topics 60
    Topics - Non Access to Text When Recording 61
Research
    Listening and Speech
        Digit and Word Recall 26
        Environment Sound 24
        Listening Range 23, 28
        Research Design 22
        Sentence Understanding 25
        Test Battery 22
        Training 22

Self-Voice Concept
    Early Findings, Children and Adults 32
    General Self-Esteem
        Links to Voice Self-Esteem 40
    Hearing Impaired Children 36
    Hearing Impaired Voices 35
    High Voice Self-Esteem Cohort 36
    Low Voice Self-Esteem Cohort 36
    Pitch Range 39
    Ranking of Adult Voices - Pilot Project 34
    Research Design 34
    Self-Voice Liking, reasons for 37
    Self-Voice Recognition Air/Bone Conduction 39
    Self-Voice Recognition Sentence 38
    Self-Voice Recognition Vowel 39
    Self-Voice Recognition Word List 38
    Test Material 35
    Voice and General Self–Esteem 40
    Voice Self-Esteem 40
Results
    Comprehension
        Comprehension Skills 69
        Independent A.R.R.O.W. Research 69
    The Vocalisation Test - Action of Story 27
    Vocalisation Test 27

S

Self-Voice
    Attitudes towards Self-Voice
        Negative Attitudes to 9
        Parent Positive Attitudes 10, 87
        Pupils' Reaction and Impact of A.R.R.O.W. to Learning Methods 11
    Chanting 56
    Defined 1
    Effects of Using the Self-Voice 37
    Internal Speech and the Self-Voice - A Running Dialogue 50
    On First Meeting the Recorded Self-Voice 6
    Rote Learning through Self-Voice Echo 48
    Self-Voice Memory Recall Tasks 50
    Superiority in Recall Tasks - Adults 50
    The Self-Voice Experience Prior to Recorded Voice Playback 5
Speech
    Adults 101, 108, 124
    Articulation Therapy 14
    Case Study Hearing Impaired 18-20
    Case Study Stroke 108
    Chanting 56
    Commendation 111
    Commendation A.R.R.O.W. Tutor 114
    Common Core Problems for Adults 103
    Early Organisation of Speech/Language Sessions 13
    National Speech Standards 56
    Pre-A.R.R.O.W. Speech and Language Improvement Strategies 9

Speech and Language Therapist Experiences 49
Split Record.. 12
Student Centred Language 61
Traditional one to one Speech Procedures 14
Vocalisation
    Vocalisation Test 27
    Vocalisation Test - Action of Story, Results.. 27
Speech and Language Therapists
    Experiences using A.R.R.O.W. 49
    Letter of Appreciation 111

T

Techniques
    Background Noise Listening Improvements.. 140
    Echoing 11, 44
        Echoic Storage of the Self-Voice 44
        Echoing 101
        Echoing and Split Record during Clinical Practice... 12
        Speech and Articulation Therapy... 14
    Free Field 61
    Grammatical Error Work.. 61
    Split Record Echoing and Split Record during Clinical Practice............................... 12
    Visual Display System.. 17
Testimonials.. 10, 12, 65, 70, 77, 78, 85, 87, 88, 91, 92, 110, 111, 114, 119, 126, 128, 129, 140, 141, 143
Text Highlighting 60
Timescales used for the Application of A.R.R.O.W.. 64
Trainer of Tutors Course 65
Training Adults in Specialised Sites
    Job Seeker Adults 122
        Basic Skills Assessments 123, 126
        Consultant Observations 124
        Driving Test Program.. 122
        Word Attack Skills... 125
    Rapid Learning 129-131
        Self-Esteem Adult's Self-Assessment of Progress 131
        Spelling Skills.. 130
        Student Selection.. 129
        Testimonials.. 129
    Specialist Residential Care Centre... 127-129
Tutor Training
    Bridgwater College 'Your Skills' A.R.R.O.W. Tutors 104
    Cascading, failure.. 58
    Early Tutor Training... 22
    Format of the Tutor Training Program.. 65
    Staff Tutor Training.. 128
    Tutor Training Procedures.. 89
Tutoring Adults Bridgwater College 'Your Skills' Course
    Adult with Autism - An Introduction 102
    Adult with Severe Learning Problems - An Introduction....................................... 100
    Adult with Traumatic Brain Injury - An Introduction 102
    Adults in Residential Homes - Group 2 111
    Adults with Alzheimer's 99

Index

Adults with Autism 129
Adults with Brain Injury - Group 4 117
Adults with CVA Stroke - Group 1 106
Adults with Severe Learning Problems - Group 3 .... 100, 115
Adults with Stroke - An Introduction 97
Adults with Stroke - Liverpool 98

U

Understanding
    Sentence Understanding Test 25

V

Vocalisation Test - Action of Story 27
Vocalisation Test and Results 27
Voluntary Societies - Role of the Voluntary Societies 8

W

Word Recall 26, 47, 50, 107, 112-119
Word Recognition (Word Attack) 72, 123, 125

Y

Young Pupils Using A.R.R.O.W.
    Groundbreaking Evidence from Years 1 and 2 72